THE STRATEGIC PLANNING GUIDE FOR EVENT PROFESSIONALS

How Strategic Events Will:
Ignite Your Career,
Transform Your Company &
Elevate the Entire Meeting Industry

CHRISTY LAMAGNA, CMP, CMM, CTSM

This is for my Dad, who inspired my love of words, reading and books.

"Quack"

Acknowledgments

When I committed to writing this book, I had no idea what it would entail, not just from me but from my amazing Strategic Meetings & Events (SME) Team. They each went from having no understanding of book publishing, marketing or design to immersing themselves in this adventure right beside me, confidently navigating the process. I am humbled by their support, loyalty, talents and boundless enthusiasm.

When my fantastic publishing coach told me that I needed to find people to join the launch team, she said that if I asked 70 people I would be lucky to get 35. I had 90 people the day after I asked for support, and it grew from there. I'm not sure what I've done to deserve that, but I'm deeply grateful and once again humbled.

This has been a collaborative effort. Colleagues, both old and new, have offered to buy, edit, contribute to, proofread, design and critique my work throughout the process, all of which have shaped the book you now hold in your hands or are reading on your screen.

My editor (and friend) jumped in a mere four weeks before the book's deadline, replacing my initial editor who had to step aside. Her edits made my words sing, and her comments inside the text made me laugh out loud when I was so bleary-eyed I could barely see the pages clearly.

When I started this journey, my goal was to give to others and inspire them. Instead, I have been overwhelmed by the generosity of those who have given so much to *me*. I am unbelievably blessed by the people in my life and thank each of you for the calls of encouragement, meals delivered, words of support, glasses of wine, and unwavering faith that this would finally be more than a dream.

Additional thanks must be given to colleagues who went above and beyond, each in their own wonderful way:

Terri Breining, Erin Buckley, Paul Collins, Holly Duckworth, Joan Eisenstodt, Charmaine Houck, Rick Hud, Phil Gerbyshak, Julian Lwin, Sanece Marie Poolas, Cody Price, James Rota, Kristi Casey Sanders, Lisa Plummer Savas, and Shawna Suckow.

A special mention to John Nawn, who co-authored chapter six, and contributed to a few others. John shared his time, wisdom and amazing templates so we may all do our jobs better. His quiet brilliance serves as a reminder of who I aspire to be.

My family and friends were instrumental in getting me to the finish line: Nancy, Kathy, Shaz, Lainie, Lynn, MC, Karin, Joe-Joe, Jack, Olivia, Stephanie, Laurie, Seth, Bruce, Linda and Eddie, Nick, Dan, Carlos, Ben, Emilia, some guy named Jeremy, my mom (of course), Keith, and so many others...

To each of you; thank you for more than I can express, but which I hope you understand.

Strategic Resource Library
How to Become a Strategic Insider

Throughout the book, you will find references to the Strategic Resource Library.

The Strategic Resource Library is a subscription-only repository for Strategic Insiders. This online resource includes templates, checklists, reference guides, best practices, as well as a vast collection of articles, blogs, and videos.

My goal for creating the Strategic Resource Library is to help you redefine excellence and incorporate what you will learn within this book into your best practices.

As a thank you for purchasing my book I am offering you a complimentary subscription to the Strategic Resource Library (valued at $499).

Claim your exclusive subscription here and become a Strategic Insider: https://members.lifelivedstrategically.com/strategic-insiders

Contents

Who Should Read This Book

Everyone can benefit from applying a strategic approach to not only their careers but also to their lives. More important than your title, years of experience, or area of the industry you're from is your desire to learn and do the work required to elevate yourself. And in that effort, there arises the opportunity to also elevate our entire industry. I write from the perspective of a senior level planner because I believe that change starts at the top. Some material may be immediately implementable, other parts you can tuck away for when you are further along in your career. It's never too early to learn and invest in your future.

✥ If you can relate to any of the following, then this book is for you:

- Are an event professional working for an organization that undervalues what you do and the events you produce

- Create events that have (the potential to have) a significant impact on sales, market share, and customer engagement for your company or your industry

- Know you add value and are good at what you do but aren't appreciated

- Are not invited to top-level marketing/sales strategy meetings

- Report to someone who has no formal event experience and who doesn't want to know or hear about event details

- Are confident that you could make major improvements in your organization's event planning process if only someone would ask you

- Rate your job satisfaction at 6 or below on a scale of 10 and wonder why you stay

This book adds perspective to a rapidly evolving industry and enables you to harness the as-yet-untapped potential of events. It doesn't matter if you consider yourself a meeting planner or an event planner; (I use the terms interchangeably throughout the book). This is your opportunity to help create what will one day be history, to be an instrumental force of change and to contribute meaningfully not just to your professional career and organization but to an entire industry. Why read about what happened when you have a chance to help *make* it happen?

Even if your professional ambitions don't include climbing the corporate ladder, using a strategic planning approach is still beneficial. When we elevate the way events are envisioned, produced and valued, everyone benefits.

Frankly, the only reason I can see to opt out of evolving into an event strategist is if everything in your professional world is exactly the way you want it to be right now.

Strategic planning removes many of the obstacles that currently impede your progress, contributes to your organization's bottom line and delivers solutions to many of the problems plaguing our industry—and that's just the beginning. *It's not magic ... it's strategic!*

Foreword

This book is designed for those who generally have more experience in designing meetings—even those who have, for years, been tasked with managing "only" the logistics of meetings and conventions. And (as we say in improvisation v. "but"!) I believe strongly that all of us are capable of being the voice presenting strategy in the process of creating and executing meetings. The principles in this book apply to those who are tasked with creating a meeting from initial conception to those who are servicing a meeting by providing the venue, the audio visual and production support, and even for speakers and entertainers who add to the delivery and outcomes for those who attend meetings. It is to help make all the stakeholders aware of the "whys" as well as the "hows" for seminar to 35,000 plus person city wide conventions regardless of one's specific role. It presents an opportunity to those whose jobs may now be considered less than strategic to look ahead and to learn to say "tell me more" and to take the improvisation trick of "yes and" to move the outcomes forward. As you read this book, open your mind to being more than you have been and to making meetings more than they have been by presenting options and having your voice heard. In the end, we all benefit from stronger, more strategic meetings.

—Joan L. Eisenstodt, Principal, Eisenstodt Associates, LLC (founded 1981)

Preface

My Goal

Life is an ongoing dance: you set goals, reach them (and sometimes reset them and try again), bask in the glory of achievement for a moment and then start anew. Each iteration gives you the opportunity to try something again, differently, or retire a goal knowing that you did your best and now consider it complete. I find that the more clearly I imagine what success looks like, the more it becomes crystalized in my mind. When the vision is so vivid I can almost touch it, an internal spark ignites my adrenaline, and POW! I'm catapulted toward making it happen.

I refer to a clear vision of success as "starting with the end in mind." It frames your perspective and reduces distraction. To keep the momentum, I also set a realistic time frame for reaching my goal and have one or more ways to measure your progress. That you are reading these words right now is itself one of the goals I set for myself: To write this book, share it with the event planning community, and start conversations that inspire change. Thank you for helping me succeed.

I set out writing this book as a way to unearth the untapped power of events and to enable industry professionals to deliver more than most imagine events are capable of. My goal is for dedicated planning professionals to be empowered and uplifted.

For those of you who want to shift your focus to a higher strategic level, this book will give you the opportunity to elevate your role within your organization, from event planner to *event strategist*, from event director to *Master Strategist*. And with this new, powerful perspective (and some practiced internal fortitude and hard work), you can also blow your organization's sales, marketing, and customer experience metrics off the charts. That's a game changer.

Also important to me (and hopefully to you, too) is moving the entire event planning industry forward and upward in importance. My idea of success for this industry is our having a shared vision, a powerful voice, and a set of goals that includes mutual support and respect and a continued dedication to improving the profession.

I am committed to seeing a strategic, transformative evolution happen within our industry within ten years from the writing of this book (so, 2028); although evolution is a never-ending process.

Growing as individual professionals and as an industry requires more than keeping up with trends and technologies. It's about (re)defining who we are, what we know, and what we know how to do. It's about setting realistic benchmarks for success. It requires delineating how we want to be treated and establishing new industry-wide standards which assure that this elevated professional status is accepted by practitioners and our clients/employers alike. It's about earning a seat at the table where key decisions are made about the very work we do. I want us to have every opportunity to develop professionally and personally.

I am even going so far as to call for mandatory licensing for strategists who plan and manage group events, where groups are defined by the industry and hotels as events with more than ten attendees.

Victory for us will be gauged on the success of our organizations in the form of creating meetings that achieve business goals and objectives. That means better sales, increased market share, higher morale, and greater collaboration, partnership quality and customer satisfaction. Organizations that adopt a strategic planning process, those who put Master Strategists on their executive leadership teams and allow event strategists to orchestrate goal-driven logistics, will go far toward achieving these results.

What's great is, should you choose to make this your goal, you can start today, right now. In fact, you already have. This book introduces you to the concepts, practices, and support tools to guide you along your transformation path to a new way of seeing, acting, and communicating.

If you want to turbo-charge your career, gain a higher sense of purpose and satisfaction from your work, and be seen as a valued contributor in your organization, then keep reading.

I've done my best to explain new ideas clearly. However, where I thought it would be useful to provide a more detailed explanation of certain words and phrases, I've bolded them, and you'll find them defined in the glossary. I also point out where to find additional information on certain topics.

What This Book Will Do for You

This book introduces event planners from all industries to the concept of strategic planning. It provides clear instructions on how to effectively incorporate strategic planning into every conversation you engage in about your work. That includes every action you take when producing events of almost any type or size.

Most examples are from my years in corporate planning, primarily serving internal audiences. However, the principles and lessons work equally well for external events or for meetings put on by professionals who don't work in a corporate setting. The key is that the book and the processes we discuss are geared toward the professional event planner. (If you're a one-time wedding planner, sorry, wrong book.)

Each chapter looks at events through a strategic lens. As you make progress and adopt this new perspective, you'll even begin to view traditional event logistics in a new way. And we'll discuss why this is so important.

This book will teach you to turn event expenditures, or "spends" in industry jargon, into investments that accelerate the sales process. You'll discover how events can help achieve business objectives and how your work can become of integral interest to the executive team.

By the book's conclusion, you will be clear on the differences between being an *event planner* and an *event strategist* and how to make the shift. If you're an *event director*, you'll learn how to evolve into a *Master Strategist*, the highest level in strategic planning hierarchy. You will have a solid foundation, tools to measure progress, and a collection of valuable resources and templates to support you along the way. And most of all, you'll be prepared to confidently introduce this concept to your executive team and get their buy-in.

I want this to be a transformational dialogue with you, and I invite you to share the concepts and materials with your colleagues, supervisors, partners, and clients.

Challenges I've faced and the lessons I've learned are openly shared so you can avoid the potholes I hit head-on. Why should we both make the same mistakes?

I also share my opinions openly. You may not agree with everything you read, but, frankly, that's part of the process. Disagreement is a healthy sign that you're engaged and processing the concepts. I welcome and encourage your feedback; learning is a two-way street.

You also have access to templates and tools that the Strategic Meetings & Events team created and uses, in the Strategic Resource Library.

Another of my objectives is to build a strong, cohesive, strategic community where we share resources, teach, mentor, inspire and encourage each other, maybe nag a little, and lift each other up. Let's start the conversation by my asking that you share with me how I can support you as you achieve *your* goals. I'd love to assist. Email me at: Christy@LifeLivedStrategically(dot)com.

Please also email any best practices and templates you've developed which you would like to share. (My team will make a point of acknowledging your cleverness when we share it.)

Pro Tip:

When you put an email address into a document, it can be searched and then used for "phishing" scams and junk mail. If you write the word "dot" as seen above, you prevent that from happening.

The Event Industry Today

"If you do not change direction, you may end up where you are heading."

~LAO TSU

Key Terms:

- ✦ Event Planning
- ✦ Events Industry Council
- ✦ Meetings Mean Business Coalition (MMBC)
- ✦ Professional Convention Management Association (PCMA)
- ✦ Meeting Professionals International (MPI)
- ✦ Certified Meeting Professional (CMP)
- ✦ Master Strategist
- ✦ Certified Meeting Management (CMM)

Event planning today is a profession predominantly driven by logistics. Event planners devote countless hours to choosing destination cities and hotels, carefully creating menus, planning receptions, selecting speakers, managing hotel accommodations, choosing décor, and a myriad of other details that create a logistically flawless onsite experience for attendees.

But meeting planning is often a task left to someone with no formal training. It's as if it was decided somewhere along the way that this was a hobby which *anyone* could instantly finesse. I wonder if an executive who puts a random person in charge of critical events would also let that person cut their hair. No way. *THAT* takes training and expertise. In truth, it's likely no one actually decided that events should be the stuff of amateurs; it's more like the situation has evolved as a matter of institutionalized neglect and a lack of attention. I've spoken to hundreds of planners, many of whom are at a loss for how the industry can be improved. I have spent my career creating, testing, and refining a plan to redefine how events are perceived and produced and how to elevate the professionals who plan them. Strategic events are the solution.

But It Looks So Simple

There are some serious misconceptions about what goes into successful meeting planning and execution, even from would-be planners themselves.

A friend who knows about my company and my work mentioned over lunch that her neighbor was very eager to meet me. She was interested in learning more about what I do. Sure, I said, and a meeting was arranged. It turned out the neighbor, Sharon, was a local mom with four kids ranging from 12 to 21, who was currently not working full-time. We sat down over iced teas and Sharon jumped right in.

She excitedly began telling me about the magnificence of her eldest daughter's wedding for 400 guests, the clever crossword puzzle invitations, the cake with edible flowers, the candlelight-colored dress with the breakaway train, and she'd planned it all herself. I smiled and nodded, a lot. I don't plan weddings and I don't have daughters, so I wasn't sure why she was telling me all this. And then it dawned on me. Sharon figured that after planning her family's birthday parties, a 50th anniversary bash for her parents, and now her eldest daughter's wedding, she was an expert event planner. Sure enough, she excitedly shared that she was thinking of opening her own event planning firm and wanted my professional advice on landing corporate clients. I asked why she'd want corporate clients if she wanted to be a party planner. She shrugged her shoulders and said: "It's all the same, right?"

I took a breath. I smiled. Then I asked Sharon if she had cooked meals for her family in the past two weeks. Of course she had. I then asked if she was also planning to open a restaurant. Let's just say things got a little awkward. But seriously, if the restaurant idea seemed absurd, then why didn't the idea of picking up a full-time corporate event planning career with no formal experience seem equally as incongruous?

The belief that anyone with a successful baby shower or surprise party under their belt can become a professional event planner is not uncommon. Based on her perception of the industry, Sharon thought she was eminently qualified to immediately be *not only a professional party planner but also a professional event planner.*

The lack of distinction between what event professionals and what party planners do is woefully lacking and must be addressed. Don't get me wrong, party planners are professionals in their own right who offer an important service. And yes, they too, can benefit from adopting a strategic approach, but they're not who I'm talking to in this book, which is geared to a much higher skill and business experience level.

As a professional event planner, it's likely that you have encountered these scenarios, too. I've been thinking about how to change these misperceptions and bring a new legitimacy and perceived value to our profession for decades. That's what led me to strategic planning. This book is the culmination of much of what I've learned. I'm sharing it with you, hoping it will inspire you to rally around a unified cause and give us all more power to be recognized for all we do and are.

How Things Have Changed ... and It Will Only Continue

Many of today's seasoned professionals learned their skills on the job, making it up as they went along. Their companies were confronted with a void; they needed someone to plan an event, and a few brave souls jumped in and saved the day. No one formally trained them, and they barely had time to plan all the events that were cropping up around them, much less create a plan for an industry. It's been an exponential parade of deadlines and logistics ever since, bringing with it a legacy of war stories and shared best practices that have forged this industry.

Curious as to just how big the industry has become? For the U.S., we draw on a 2018 report from Oxford Economics, which was commissioned by the **Events Industry Council** and supported by the **Meetings Mean Business Coalition** and other industry partners. Oxford Economics compiled responses from a nationwide survey of meeting planners, exhibitors, and venues. The resulting report represents the opinions of almost 9,000 domestic business travelers, nearly 50,000 international air travelers, and 11,000 hotels.

According to Adam Sacks, founder and president of Tourism Economics, an Oxford Economics company, "The meetings and events industry continues to grow across all segments as it contributes hundreds of billions [of dollars] in revenue to the U.S. economy and supports 5.9 million jobs. Notably, in 2016, meetings generated $325 billion of direct spending and $845 billion in business sales. These numbers represent a contribution of $446 billion in GDP and $104 billion of federal, state, and local taxes."

That report goes on to say that a total of 1.9 million meetings were held in 2016, with 251 million participants. And this is just for the U.S. market.

These figures are staggering considering how young the industry is. The **Professional Convention Management Association (PCMA)**, the granddaddy of industry associations, held its first convention in 1956. (Ironically, the number of people with enough budget to travel to its own event was small.)

In 1972, when the **Meeting Professional International (MPI)** organization was formed, computers that could fit on a desk were just beginning to appear on the scene, but not many people knew how to use them. There were no Excel files to help quickly make a program of events (POE) or build a line-item budget with automated formulas. The **Certified Meeting Planner (CMP)** designation wasn't introduced until 1985, and the **Certification in Meeting Management (CMM)** until 1998.

When I got started, formal resources were still rather scarce. It took long hours, lots of phone calls, and countless rolls of duct tape to craft flawless events. The Internet didn't become mainstream until 1995.

The prime motivation for this book is that, even today, with all the resources we have at our fingertips, most industry professionals still use a logistics-based planning model rather than a strategic one. This prevents events and event planners themselves from achieving their full potential.

Until we employ a strategic approach and do the work required to earn the title of event strategist and **Master Strategist**, we cannot fully realize what we or the events we work so hard to design are fully capable of.

We are at a crossroads. We must establish new, shared processes, standards, systems and entry requirements, for established professionals as well as new practitioners who are ready to earn a seat at the table.

Designing Our Future

Traditional corporate hierarchies today have some standard positions at the top: CEO, COO, CMO, CFO. Some even have a chief strategy officer. And then there are the executive vice presidents of each function, including sales. Each has a critical and distinct role in the organization. Their success is measured in large part by their organization's profitability and contribution to the overall bottom line. One untapped resource for boosting a company's competitive edge and bottom line revenue is identifying and promoting a Master Strategist to the ranks of their executive team.

Master Strategists become the binding agent between sales, marketing, and event departments. These highly skilled individuals design event environments that bring marketing messages to life and influence what a target audience thinks, says, and does after the meeting. Master Strategists are trained experts under whose direction meetings become vehicles that help drive sales and other important business goals.

When I shifted from a logistics-based planning perspective to a strategic one I no longer struggled to get the budget dollars I needed to properly host events. My exhausting 16-hour days with little validation were replaced with inclusion on the executive team and a new-won respect for me, my staff and our work. Not only that, but my *strategic* event planning team got more meaning out of their work, had fewer interoffice power struggles, increased their quality of life, reduced their workload, and boosted their salaries. I'm not kidding! The difference is profound.

Strategic planning transforms organizations that host events by turning those events into powerful tools which deliver a positive, bottom-line impact. They typically cost less, and the dollars allocated to them are seen as investments rather than expenses. It's a win, win, win. A win for those organizations that choose to invest in the strategic process, a win for the strategists who design these better events and gain the edge they seek and respect they deserve, and a win for customers who benefit from events better tailored to their needs.

We've Got the Power

Planners are logistical geniuses and supreme multi-taskers. We're calm under pressure, tireless, and a long list of other formidable adjectives. Yet many of us feel unfulfilled and under-appreciated. It's easy to blame it on management. But, for change to take place, we need to look inward and transform the way we think about, discuss, and execute events.

As we've established, events are typically driven by logistics. To executives, logistics are noise. Executives think and measure success in broad brush strokes: increased revenues, lower costs, a bigger slice of market share. Executive's minds truly don't want to be bothered with logistical details. That's why they hired us. But there's a huge piece missing.

For event planners, logistics are typically our primary focus. If we shift our perspective upward and view events in the bigger business context, *which is what strategic event thinking is all about*, we raise the importance of events to a new level. Strategic events achieve business goals and objectives, add measurable value to the organization, and reduce the cost to produce them. Strategists have the power to turn event budgets into business gold.

Trusting the Mechanics of Applied Strategy

There is a defined and purposeful process to strategic meetings and to measuring their results. In the world of strategic planning, having anyone but a trained, certified, or licensed professional producing your events would be like having your pet sitter perform your root canal. Cheaper, sure, but inadvisable over the long haul.

The cost of materials, salaries, and travel are soaring. Competition for market share is fierce. Successful companies are the ones who recognize and harness the power of strategic events to help drive sales performance. And event strategists know how to make that happen. This not only provides job security, but also elevates the role to one which carries direct responsibility for achieving the organization's most fundamental and important goals and objectives.

"Until we employ a strategic approach and do the work required, we cannot fully realize what we or events are capable of."

~ CHRISTY LAMAGNA

CHAPTER ONE

Beyond Logistics: Setting Our Sights on Strategy

"Others have seen what is and asked why.
I have seen what could be and asked why not."

~PABLO PICASSO

Key Terms for This Chapter:

- ✧ Event Strategist
- ✧ Event Planner
- ✧ Smart Badges

Traditional planning starts with logistics, or the HOW of events: How are we going to feed 30 people on a budget for 12? How are we going to flip the ballroom from theatre seating to rounds for 500 in 30 minutes? How can we get 27,000 LED-festooned Mickey Mouse hats distributed to a stadium audience in 20 minutes?

Event strategy, on the other hand, requires that you first answer WHY. Why is the meeting being held in the first place? Based on the goals established in the strategic plan, what goal will this meeting be designed to support or achieve? It doesn't matter if this is the 10th annual meeting you've planned for the sales team, you must always seek out the WHY with a fresh perspective. "Because we have it every year" is not an answer, by the way. If you skip this step—thinking the WHY is the same every year—you are setting yourself up for unnecessary trouble. It's a huge red flag.

Event strategists rely on research and a lot of data to design immersive experiences that carry a high probability of satisfying both stakeholders and audiences. (We will discuss this in detail in Chapter 6.) They not only produce successful individual events, they effectively support and accelerate measurable sales and marketing goals.

The process always begins with the end in mind. That is, starting with the outcomes you want to achieve and working backwards to determine the inputs and actions needed to reach them. When goals aren't met, everyone ends up unhappy, which is something many of you can likely relate to and want to avoid at all cost. Consider this example:

> *Castle House Productions, which provides event gear and ballroom production services, is facing plummeting sales, and profits are at an all-time low. The sales meeting is coming up, but rumors are that it may be canceled. Despite numerous emails and conversations, the* **event planner**, *Jack, can't get a solid confirmation from the VP of sales and is worried about missing the next cancellation date, which means big losses.*

> *Jack finally gets the word that the meeting will happen but learns from the CEO's executive assistant, Olivia, that it will focus on the launch of a new inventory control software system which will boost sales. It will require that a trainer be onsite for four hours of on boarding. This is impossible given the meeting's current schedule, Jack is thinking as she talks. Then Olivia adds that the executives now want to add an extra half-day to accommodate the training. Wow. Everyone else thinks this solves all the issues. For Jack, it creates a whole cascade of new ones.*

> *His to-do list is already a mile long and now he must jump through hoops to adjust the plan and accommodate an extra half day. How can a decision like this be made without him in the room? Don't they understand the difference between having an idea and executing it?*

> *What if the hotel can't extend its hold time on the ballroom and breakout space? Is the production team available for an extra day? Can they extend the hotel room block to accommodate attendees who won't be able to fly out as*

planned? Where is the money going to come from to cover the extra costs if the changes can be made? Jack sighs and gets busy. Fortunately, it turns out he can make the required changes.

The events team has been busy designing a "Tracking Our Progress" theme. Among other plans, **smart badges** will help attendees network with colleagues and let the planning team know who attends which sessions. The theme and logistics tie in perfectly to the software launch. Everyone is excited about how the plan has jelled.

Meanwhile, the COO calls together a committee to begin researching the new software solution. Four months and countless meetings later, a vendor is chosen, and the investment looks promising. The state-of-the-art software tracks inventory and streamlines equipment rentals, eliminating downtime and maximizing the usage of the company's gear. The price is steep, but based on the metrics, the returns will offset the spend in two years. The C-Suite buys in, the mood around the table is optimistic.

At the big sales event, the CEO kicks it off with a rousing entrance to flashing lights and pounding music—his fist pumping the air as he jogs to center stage. After giving a general state of the union, he announces the software roll-out. The cutting-edge software will let the sales team see inventory in real time, allowing for more sell-through, he enthuses. That means more sales, more commissions, less paperwork, more selling!

The CEO is proud of his investment in the sales force. Lesser leaders might have used the meeting as a platform to threaten layoffs, reduce commissions and increase quotas. But this executive team is instead investing in its employees. He raises his arms in a motion that communicates how proud and magnanimous he feels.

Surprisingly, applause for the CEO is tepid and the energy in the room tanks. The CEO is confused and reads this response as a lack of appreciation. "What more could these people want?" he wonders defensively. The CEO and executive team are in a foul mood for the rest of the meeting. Attendees are disengaged, and the training is painful. During breaks, the planners overhear grumbling that the whole meeting is a waste of time. The meeting limps to a close. The executives exit as a dejected pack, befuddled and discouraged.

Later, attendees grade the event poorly on the feedback survey. With negative feedback from both sides, Jack and his team are deflated and exhausted. On paper, it seemed like it should have been a perfect event. But no one is happy.

Shifting the Lens to Strategic Thinking

If this sounds all too familiar, it's not surprising. But it's also great news: if situations like this are happening now, you'll be glad to know that we're going to put the pieces in place here for you to make a 180-degree shift in your work, your career, and your organization's events. It all starts with a strategic plan. The good news is that it's likely your company already has one in place. The bad news is, so far you haven't been part of it, but that's about to change.

"Traditional planning starts with logistics.
Strategic planning starts with asking why."

~ CHRISTY LAMAGNA

CHAPTER TWO

Understanding the WHY

"Don't agonize, organize."

~FLORYNCE KENNEDY

Key Terms for This Chapter:

- ✦ Strategic Plan
- ✦ Goals
- ✦ Objectives
- ✦ Tasks
- ✦ Strategic Planning
- ✦ Discovery Process
- ✦ Master Discovery Session®
- ✦ Discovery Sessions
- ✦ Data Discovery®
- ✦ Strategic Content Creation®
- ✦ Post-Show Metrics, Audits and Reviews
- ✦ Post-mortem
- ✦ Event Objectives Calendar®
- ✦ FOMO
- ✦ Pop-up Meetings

When executed strategically, events are critical stepping stones towards achieving an organization's goals. The first step is knowing what those goals are and how they are set. This info is in your company's **strategic plan.**

A strategic plan is an organizational tool that helps to keep a company on track to meet growth and financial objectives. Strategic plans envision a desired future and translate the vision into broadly defined goals, objectives, and tasks.

All businesses, regardless of what they sell or what services they provide, aim to maximize profits, minimize expenses, and grow market share. The formal statement of those goals is encapsulated in a strategic plan. Any department or individual who contributes positively to the attainment of these targets is considered an asset to the organization. Unlike traditional events, which are logistical in their approach, strategic events are designed to achieve business goals and objectives, which should earn them a place in the strategic plan.

Goals vs. Objectives

In daily conversation, we use the terms "goals" and "objectives" interchangeably. When executing a strategic plan there is an important distinction. Both lead you to the desired outcome, but each plays a specific role.

Goals are the big picture, the overarching vision. When we talk about "starting with the end in mind," the end is the goal.

Objectives are integral to achieving a goal. Objectives are specific, short-term actions that advance towards the goal. For our purposes, events are objectives. Objectives require answers to *WHO*, *WHAT*, *WHEN*, *WHERE*, *WHY* and *HOW*.

The WHY is the event's purpose, which is to move the organization a step closer to the goals outlined in the strategic plan.

Tasks are the steps or activities performed to complete the objectives. Tasks are the event logistics behind the meeting.

Master Discovery Sessions

Strategic plans are usually created in meetings at a senior-executive or board-of-directors level. The goals established in those meetings give everyone guidelines on where to focus their attention and actions.

Chances are these goals were even discussed during the annual sales meeting. They shouldn't be hard to get your hands on (top-secret-goals are great for spy movies, but not so much for effective corporate strategy). The assistant to the EVP of sales or anyone on the sales team should be able to share a copy.

Once you review the strategic plan and understand what your company's goals and objectives are, your part in helping to achieve them begins. Adopting a strategic approach starts off simply by having access to pertinent information and then gathering the right people to act upon it. It may feel like it should be more complicated than that but it's not. Once you have the goals and objectives, your **strategic planning** begins. It's all encompassed in the **Discovery Process**.

✧ The Discovery Process has five main steps:

1. **Master Discovery Session** - an initial session in which to assign goals and objectives to each event

2. **Discovery Sessions** – sessions held for each event to establish how the event will meet its objective

3. **Data Discovery** – a process that will help you gather critical audience info

4. **Strategic Content Creation** – content identified as supporting the objectives

5. **Post-show metrics, audits, and reviews** – the **post-mortem** where you see how well you did and learn lessons to apply to future events

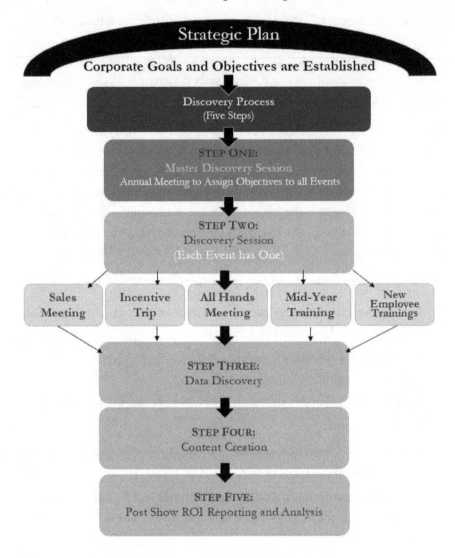

The Master Discovery Session®

The purpose of the Master Discovery Session is to assign specific objectives to each event that falls within the strategic plan's timeline. It requires getting the right executives in the room, which may be a challenge initially, but I'll give you suggestions for how to do that successfully.

One of many tangible products from a Master Discovery Session is an **Event Objectives Calendar**. Unlike a traditional event calendar, which

details names, dates, locations, and other event logistics, an Event
Objectives Calendar also identifies target audiences and established
objectives. It's a simple and effective way to keep everyone focused on
the purpose of the meeting. It can be distributed to sales, marketing,
strategic events teams, and to all other appropriate departments via
email. You may even want to post the schedule on your company's
internal site. (Knowledge is power.) Here's an example:

Castle House Productions Event Objectives Calendar

Start Date	End Date	Event	Audience	Objective	Supported Goal
Feb-3	Feb-5	Sales meeting	Sales team	Provide sales tools, drive sales	Increase sales, capture market share, lower turnover
Ap-9	Apr-13	Incentive trip	Qualifiers from entire organization	Recognize achievements. Build morale, create **FOMO** for organization.	Increase sales, capture additional revenue
Jun-1	Jun-2	Mid-Year training	Department Managers	Best practices reviewed, skills/ tools introduced and taught	Lower customer turnover
May 27	May 27	All Hands meeting	Entire organization	Business outlook, update on goals, inspire, motivate	Lower customer turnover
Quarterly (1st day)		New hire training	All employees hired in the last three months	Introduce strategic plan, goals, best practices, corporate culture, vision, mission, goals, objectives	Increase sales, capture market share, lower turnover

Pro Tip:

With a master event strategy in place, you can effectively assess unanticipated requests to participate in or host "**pop-up meetings**" that arise during the year. The path has been defined and the destination is clear, which takes emotion and politics out of the process. If it doesn't fit in the plan, it shouldn't be happening.

Once people experience the difference strategic planning makes and can see measurable results, they won't just support it, they'll *embrace* it. Master Discovery Sessions and Event Objectives Calendars are standard elements of the strategic events process. From there, you are ready to schedule a discovery session.

"Any department or individual who contributes positively to the attainment of an organization's goals is an asset."

~ CHRISTY LAMAGNA

CHAPTER THREE

Preparing for Your First Discovery Session

"I didn't get to where I am by wishing for it,
or hoping for it, but by working for it.
~Estee Lauder

Key Terms for This Chapter:

✧ Key Stakeholders

✧ Strategic Vision Team®

✧ First Right Refusal

✧ Target Audience

✧ Event Design

Assembling the Strategic Vision Team

A Discovery Session is not a kickoff meeting. It is not intended to brainstorm themes or discuss destinations and venues. It is not about budgets. What it is, is a foray into the context that surrounds a meeting. Why at this time and place, for this audience, focused on this content, for what important outcomes? What metrics will measure success, and what are each stakeholder's roles and responsibilities?

Discovery Sessions are invitation-only meetings attended by **key stakeholders**, many of whom would likely have been in the Master Strategy Meeting. This group is your "**Strategic Vision Team.**"

To determine who makes the invitation list, think about whose budget underwrites the event and/or where the blame lands if the event tanks. Unless your event or organization is exceptionally large, there should be no more than five people including you. Six, if you have a designated (silent) note taker. Those who attend become the key drivers throughout the event's lifespan.

✧ Strategic Vision Teams usually consist of:

- The Master Strategist
- Chief Executive Officer (CEO)
- Executive Vice President (EVP) of Sales
- Chief Marketing Officer (CMO)
- Chief Operating Officer (COO)
- Chief Financial Officer (CFO)

To successfully host a discovery session, you must do on a micro-level what you are going to do for the overall event on a macro-level. Your first discovery session is going to require a few additional steps because you need to get the executive team on board. They may consider the Master Strategy Session all that was needed. That's a great beginning but it's just that, a beginning.

So how are you going to get these people in a room and make this happen? You create and carry out your own strategic plan. This takes some upfront work, which means finding time in your already over-scheduled day, but the short-term investment will yield long-term, permanent gains.

Your goal: Bring strategic event planning to your organization

Objectives: Comprehensive adoption plan developed and implemented

Task: In-depth analysis of financial opportunities

Scheduling the first discovery session may take some extra assertiveness as well as preparation. You're adding another meeting to already overbooked calendars. You may lack direct access to the very executives who should be in attendance and the gravitas to get them to agree to be there. But what you DO have (after reading this book) is a powerful case to be made for bringing event strategy into your organization.

The Master Strategist (you) calls the meetings, sets the agenda, and drives the process. The discovery session formally puts an objective in motion. A series of follow-up meetings will be scheduled to keep the plan moving forward and handle any high-level situations that need to be addressed. The Strategic Vision Team is focused on how event objectives are supporting the organization's goals. They are the key stakeholders. They are not involved in the tasks associated with the objectives; if your Strategic Vision Team starts delving into menus and giveaway items the process isn't working.

There may be initial questions asking if these meetings are necessary. They are. Without the information gleaned through Discovery Sessions, events are a collection of cobbled-together logistics, potentially uncoordinated content, and limited ROI metrics. Basically, exactly where you are now.

✧ Discovery Sessions:

- Establish specific event objectives
- Create a common plan, vision, and vocabulary among key stakeholders
- Create clear, intentional direction
- Eliminate miscommunication
- Reduce or eliminate wasteful and/or unnecessary spending

The best way to approach the soon-to-be members of your Strategic Vision Team may vary by individual. Informally introducing the idea in conversation may be ideal for some; if your CEO eats lunch in the employee cafeteria to remain accessible, consider pulling up a chair. Perhaps you see the VP of marketing at a monthly internal meeting; use that as an opportunity to introduce the idea.

Not sure how to start the conversation? Numbers speak volumes. Chapter 6 details what data can be collected immediately by analyzing past event spending. This may be enough to open the door to the conversation and get the first Discovery Session scheduled. We will detail the tactical components of that meeting and its goals. We'll also discuss how to break through the noise and get the meeting on the calendar.

For those of you who don't have access to company executives, or for whom in-person side conversations aren't an option, take inventory of who you know who can open those doors for you. See about having them arrange for a quick presentation of your plan.

Whether you can speak to all, some, or none of your targeted stakeholders, they must all receive a succinct email that grabs their attention and summarizes the meeting's purpose *in their terms*. Executives generally focus on bottom-line revenue and costs. If you state the reason for the Discovery Session meeting and the need for their participation in a potential increase hard-dollar revenues and significant cost savings (gained through a strategic approach to events), that should get them to the table.

You may want to send the initial invitation out to the executive leadership team while you are still preparing, if you think it will take some time to get the Discovery Session scheduled. If you anticipate a quick reply, be ready with a few optional dates for this important meeting.

Digging for Data

Strategic plans create goals centered around maximizing profits, minimizing expenses, and growing market share. The logistics data you likely already have at your disposal supports potential cost reduction, so that's where to start.

Review the last three years of budgets for events and identify charges that can be linked back to key decision makers missing deadlines and creating delays. Include a list of lost opportunities. These may include missed sponsorship opportunities, first choice of venues, premium space at an event. These costs may be hard to calculate, but an estimate will be useful (be sure to indicate your assumptions in arriving at the figure). Seeing that in black and white (or rather, in red) may inspire some re-prioritizing.

◇ For example:

- A delayed decision on the giveaway item caused the missed deadlines to get the items in time and generated rush fees.

- The room release date came and went without confirmation causing extra room charges.

- Another group challenged your first-choice event space that was being held on "**first right refusal.**" The approval to contract the space was received long past the deadline and the space was lost. The second choice option which cost more and had a smaller ballroom became the only option.

Other examples of the many costs and missed opportunities planning strategically will help reduce or eliminate include late fees, rush charges, overtime, change fees, cancellation fees, attrition penalties, missed early-bird discounts, increased airfare due to last-minute bookings, second choices on merchandise, and fewer options for speakers and venues on priority dates.

The information you are gathering is NOT about trying to cut budgets. It's about improving the efficiency and performance of meetings. It's about boosting satisfaction for attendees. It's about providing measurable results to executives surrounding an event's performance. It's about contributing in a new and meaningful way to your organization and earning more respect.

The opportunities are endless. Use your imagination or talk to your company's business development team to come up with a list of potential opportunities that events provide. These may include specific ways to achieve certain partnership milestones, garner free publicity to offset marketing costs, or bring together your R&D department with the extended supply/value chain to accelerate the sales cycle.

Data Drives Tasks that Support Objectives that Achieve Goals

Data can be both quantitative (number, percentages) and qualitative (value, satisfaction, mind share). Identifying what your **target audience** needs and addressing those pain points shapes content. Creating an environment for effective learning is part of what makes up successful **event design**. Any facts that pertain to what you can do to make events better are facts you should look for and include in Discovery Sessions as well.

Creating the optimal setting for your Discovery Sessions also requires data about your executive attendees. Ask executive assistants about the work styles and personal preferences of their executives.

✧ Helpful details include:

- What time of day are they most productive?
- What day of the week is optimal for scheduling meetings?
- What does the executive like to drink? (Be specific.)
- Do they have any dietary restrictions?
- What kind of dessert or snack do they prefer? Fruit or sweets? Chocolate or something crunchy and salty?
- Ask assistants for any other helpful details they can share.

✧ Some things to consider:

- If you find out that most invitees prefer an afternoon meeting, but your CEO likes mornings, you may want to do what makes the big boss happy—or go with *majority rules* if that's the company culture.
- Keep snacks as simple as possible and seek those in wrappers that don't make a lot of noise to minimize distractions.
- If you can reserve a conference or boardroom, do it. If there is one that has natural light, even better. This allows you to arrive early to prepare, puts everyone on neutral ground and takes executives out of their offices, which also reduces distractions.
- You have a full agenda and a limited amount of time to get through it, so make sure you have your ducks in a row and are ready to keep the group focused and moving forward.

It's Showtime!

Once the executive team arrives, be ready to impress. You'll need a powerful story and compelling data to back it up if you want to get the best results. This is your time to shine. Be succinct and confident. Here are some talking points to keep in mind as you share the story of why strategic events matter:

✧ Strategic events...

- help achieve business goals and objectives
- turn event expenditures into investments
- eliminate unnecessary spending
- support and shorten sales cycles
- influence what the company's target audiences feel, think, say, and do
- improve efficiency
- are the only 3D embodiment of the company's marketing message
- build meaningful face-to-face relationships

You must believe deep in your bones that there is a meaningful distinction between logistically and strategically driven events. If you can't speak passionately about it, you're not ready to start the conversation. For even more information, go to the Strategic Resource Library for videos, webinars, suggested readings and articles to augment your strategic knowledge and help you prepare.

First, you can warm up the group with an introduction of what strategic event planning is all about and some of the generic benefits: hard cost savings, greater overall satisfaction, new revenue opportunities. You can use the talking points above to create an outline.

Then you can rely on your research to tailor these observations to your company's challenges and goals. Provide data to illustrate and support suggestions for revenue generating or cost savings opportunities.

Go to the Strategic Resource Library for a high-level view of revenue sources (or value generators, which is more inclusive of intangible benefits) and costs that you could cite as missing or in excess at your organization's past events.

Next Steps

Your first Discovery Session introduced a strong case for making changes. An immediate request for action may be met with, "Give us some time to think on it." Acknowledge that, but promptly ask to set a follow-up meeting for, say, two weeks hence. Leaving the date for the follow up open undermines the power of your argument that these changes are important and need to be addressed right away. It also makes scheduling the next meeting more difficult.

For the next two weeks, you may get questions. That's great. It's a sign they're thinking about the concepts you presented. You may want to buy them this book. In it, you can highlight the sections that most clearly addressed your organization's challenges. In fact, consider getting one for every member of the Strategic Vision Team as a way of introducing these concepts. (If you do, email me and I'll send you a discount code. This is important information that can be challenging to communicate.) Having the book in hand is a way for the team to absorb the information at their own pace. By bookmarking and highlighting the parts you found most applicable, you can help the team get to "the good parts" and align with your thinking more quickly. The sooner everyone gets on the same page, the sooner goals can be achieved.

"If your strategic vision team is focusing on menus and giveaway items the process isn't working."

~ Christy Lamagna

CHAPTER FOUR

Mapping Out the Plan

"Don't wait for opportunity. Create it."

~DEBASISH MRIDHA, M.D.

Key Terms for This Chapter:

- ✧ Impulse Answers
- ✧ SMART Goals
- ✧ Key Performance Indicators (KPIs)
- ✧ Action Plan
- ✧ Action Items
- ✧ Pain Points

When the decision has been made to move forward, an "official" Discovery Session takes place. This session focuses on a single event. Your first discovery was a trial run designed to get executive buy-in. Follow the same guidelines as you used for the first and add- or change any details you noticed needing fine tuning in the previous meeting.

This may be the first time anyone has been formally asked to contemplate events in terms of high-level goals and objectives. It's up to you to lead the conversation and keep the process moving forward.

✧ Here are some things you need to establish before any planning begins:

- What do you want attendees to feel, say, think, and do after the event?
- What behaviors are you trying to encourage or change?

- What do you want to happen because of this meeting? Be specific.

Discovery Sessions bring the event's key stakeholders together to create a unified vision for a meeting.

Remember Jack from Castle House? Here's what happened when he held his first Discovery Session:

Jack started by listing Castle House's strategic goals for the year. They were:

- *Increase sales by 10% in the next nine months*

- *Capture an additional 5% of market share*

- *Lower customer turnover by 15%*

Jack first got confirmation from everyone that these were the sales objectives as established during the Master Discovery Session. When he said he wanted to go around the table to ask each person what they thought the goals for the annual sales meeting were, their WHY for its taking place, the CEO interrupted. He didn't think it was necessary to waste time with this; the team was unified on their vision for the annual sales meeting.

Jack paused.

On the surface, key decision makers may agree on the objectives, but each likely has his or her own perspective, agenda, and priorities. Everyone comes to the table with responsibilities as they relate to the strategic goals which influence their opinions. You need consensus or, at the very least, a discussion on what the meeting should accomplish and how it can be successful on its own and in the broader context.

It may take some digging to determine the inputs and calculations to find the final answer. You'll need to learn how to differentiate between genuine and **impulse answers**. It's not uncommon for it to take a few tries before attendees get to their final answers. But first, you have to ask.

What *isn't* said is also critical. If you listen and watch attentively, you will become aware of body language: who is overly defensive, who is leaning forward, who isn't making eye contact, who hasn't said a word. At this stage, it's wise to only lightly moderate the discussion, but not become deeply involved or add opinions yourself.

It's imperative that the group hears each other and finds their way to a set of answers. Let *them* determine the goals and objectives of the meeting. Your role is to make sure the final product hits its target.

It may take more than one conversation to come to a consensus, which is actually a good sign. If people are communicating, even loudly, that means they are thinking and are emotionally invested-in the conversation. That's a long way from not reading your emails or returning your calls. To note; if the whole meeting happens in 20 minutes the plan isn't being seriously considered.

> *Jack respectfully asked that the CEO allow him to continue with the exercise. He states that giving each person the opportunity to share their vision was truly part of the process and critical to getting the results they wanted.*
>
> *The CEO acquiesced and here is what they all learned:*
>
> *The CEO wants the annual sales meeting to focus on revenue growth and market expansion. She wants the sales team to recognize that a great deal of work must be done to meet year-end goals. She believes bringing in new software and investing in training will streamline the post-order process and help achieve the desired results.*
>
> *As part of a branding overhaul, the CMO wants to fast-track re-branding the corporate website and relaunch it at the meeting. Greater functionality and a new back-end system will, among other things, let clients check order status, and review their purchasing history. This project, which he has been working on for over a year, is the key to increased customer satisfaction and follow-on sales.*

The sales EVP sees the annual meeting as the ideal place to announce to the field an expanded commission structure designed to further reward top performers, incentivize mid-level performers, and encourage the low-level performers to step up or step out.

After the EVP finished speaking, the group looked at each other a bit befuddled. They each had different objectives for the sales meeting and some were at odds with one another. No one had ever actually gone through this exercise before. Jack had proved his point.

If key decision makers are not in alignment on what success looks like, how can it be achieved? Even if they were in sync, not all of the visions were focused on the event's stated primary objective which should have aligned with the goals outlined in the Strategic Plan. This is one of the single most significant flaws of logistics-based planning. Communication is lacking and there is no clearly defined and agreed upon definition of success.

With these differences of opinion out in the open, productive discussion ensued. The final decision on the annual sales meeting's objectives was threefold.

1) They would focus on ways to increase profits and would bring in a well-regarded motivational speaker to help.

2) They would launch the new inventory management software system and

3) They would roll out the new sales compensation plan.

Great! They had clear objectives and alignment. Once these are established, make sure the necessary supporting elements are also in place. These correspond to the generally well-known goal setting acronym **SMART**, for specific, measurable, accountable, realistic, and timely. For a detailed look at SMART goals, head to the Strategic Resources Library.

In addition to SMART goals, incorporate as many of the following as you can into your plan. Each step is geared toward designing successful events.

Establish a defined and realistic time-frame to gauge results: Events can and will influence behavior, but they are not magic bullets. On average, it takes more than two months before a new behavior becomes automatic. Make sure you build in enough time before you measure so you capture real results.

Identify Key Performance Indicators (KPIs): Measure changes in critical, quantifiable variables; sales numbers, attendance numbers, and reorder numbers, that demonstrate how effectively a company is achieving its key business objectives.

Set the strategies and tactics to achieve objectives and goals: A strategy is an **action plan** for achieving a stated objective centered on an organization's next big moves or goals (strengthening customer focus, becoming more competitive, updating the company image, for instance). Tactics are the steps to achieve the goal (create a customer advisory board and bring advisors together at the annual sales meeting, prepare an event campaign to end-of-life an outdated product line, and introduce a new one that serves the existing market better or taps a new one, etc.).

Assign responsibilities and measure accountability: Defining roles and responsibilities for each member of the Strategic Vision Team is critical to achieving your objectives. There are a lot of busy people in the room, all of whom are used to the planner doing all the work when it comes to events. But that has to change. The strategist leads the process but is not the only facilitator. Carve out tasks that each member of the Strategic Vision Team is uniquely qualified and able to carry out. Determine what tasks can be done in-house and which must be outsourced is often part of this process. Whether you create an event dashboard, use calendar reminders, or create another system that works for your team, being accountable for the strategic process should be seen as of equal importance with any other prioritized tasks associated with sales and company growth.

Create a follow-up plan to support the team in achieving the goals and stick to it: Meeting notes that capture "**action items**" for individuals along with their due dates help keep people on track. Regularly scheduled meetings for the same date and time may maximize attendance. People want to know what is expected of them and when. The event strategy team is going to do the heavy lifting. The Strategic Vision Team weighs in on decisions that affect the objectives or on items that increase spend and require authorization.

With an understanding of what the objectives are and the support tools in place to measure them, Jack's next step in the discovery process is Data Discovery. Once the WHY of the meeting is confirmed, you will create the plan for how to deliver those results.

The only way to develop truly relevant content is to clearly understand the target audience's **pain points** and concerns. This information comes from Data Discovery. This step determines the WHAT, as in what the target audience needs to hear, learn, or do to improve performance. When performance improves, positive results follow.

Understanding what to ask, how to ask it, and who to speak to is the next step in the process.

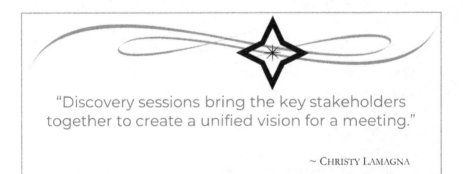

"Discovery sessions bring the key stakeholders together to create a unified vision for a meeting."

~ Christy Lamagna

CHAPTER FIVE

Ask Them and Ye Shall Get an Earful

"The more I learn, the more I realize how much I don't know."

~ALBERT EINSTEIN

Let's revisit what we've established thus far so we may confidently get to the next steps.

✧ When properly executed, strategic events can:

- Achieve or assist in reaching the company's business goals by shortening sales cycles

- Bring marketing messages to life

- Influence what your attendees feel, think, say, and do

When events don't have predetermined and clearly stated objectives, they can't be deemed successful. Without defining the event's WHY you have no destination, as to the WHERE. If you don't know where you're going how will you know when you've arrived?

Let's look at the anatomy of the WHY. The WHY is 50 percent want (what executives want) and 50 percent need (what the target audience needs). Currently, most events are announced, planners scramble to find dates and space, create a budget, and cobble together the pieces to do what was asked. To the organization's detriment, events are almost always planned without meaningful input from the target audience. This stems from a pervasive sense that management already knows what their target audience is thinking or what executives want to say directly correlates with what attendees need to hear. That often turns out to be "non-sense." And at 50 percent of the success equation, that's dangerous.

Just asking past attendees for their destination preferences for next year or whether they like the prime rib at the customer appreciation dinner will not provide the necessary input for a valid Strategic Plan. We need to explore the context around the event and ask more comprehensive questions to a broader set of responders. Until we better understand attendees' needs, we won't know whether the event's content is adequate. That could mean it applies to their day-to-day work, allows them to reach new customers, solves a major problem they have and, ultimately, changes their behavior in a direction we desire. If we don't know this, then we can't plan strategically.

So, be sure you're selecting and sequencing your input sources effectively and strategically: After you hear from executives and other internal stakeholders, make time to connect with your target audience and ask for their input. If you skip this step, you almost guarantee failure or only tactical success. Let's look at how this translates to everyday life.

This is Not What I Ordered

A toy store in my neighborhood closed, leaving an empty building in the town's downtown shopping area. My friends and I speculated on what would take its place. A few hoped for a health food store, and others wanted a yogurt shop, a bakery, or a juice bar. Since it is a small town and we were likely to patronize whatever went in, we felt somewhat entitled to be in on the decision. Unfortunately, before anyone asked, we learned that a small, exclusive restaurant would be moving into the space. Frankly, we were disappointed. Given the number of restaurants already in town, this didn't seem like a good fit.

While it had a certain appeal, it didn't feel very accessible to us locals. The owners had imported everything, the chefs, the bartenders, and even the wait staff, from New York City. They'd been sure that a swanky Manhattan-style dining experience was just what the neighborhood needed. For us residents, though, we found the snooty reservation policy, the tiny portions, and the close proximity of the tables off-putting. The prices were too high, and we were offended by the lack of local hires. It closed 18 months later. The owners lost a bundle.

They could have saved that bundle if they had asked for our input. While we may not have represented their entire target market, we certainly could have been an easily reachable niche with the potential to help them build a following. But they missed the opportunity to connect with the neighborhood early in the decision-making process and so lost our approval and endorsement. As it turns out, it was a fatal mistake.

Successful entrepreneurs research what their target audiences want, need, and are willing to support. Yes, they may take some liberties to create something innovative, but they must find out attendee pain points and identify ways to address them. The same is true for events. Ask a sampling of attendees who they want to hear, what they need to learn, or what they hope to experience, and they'll tell you. If you then share that information with the Strategic Vision Team and build the event content around those needs, you equip your planners with the tools and information they can use to achieve the goals established in the Discovery Session.

The Top, Middle, and Bottom

Optimally performing sales teams are rainmakers. Ensuring they have what they need to succeed seems like an obvious proviso. Yet many executives impede their sales force by assuming, often incorrectly, what their employees or customers want and build out the strategy based on those poor assumptions. It's possible that executives believe they can speak for their sales team because they were once in their shoes. But are they still? Sales environments change rapidly and getting accurate, timely feedback is essential to understanding the true needs and wants of your audience.

Typically, sales organizations have performers who range from a small group of rock stars, a larger percentage of mid-level performers, and then a group of those who can't quite get it together. If you ask someone at each performance level; What hinders your success? What do you need to be more productive? Happier? More fulfilled? What would you change if you were in charge?—you will get an interesting array of answers.

Each question addresses a need, state of mind, or unfulfilled wish. And here's where it gets very rich: This is where you can deliver a powerful payoff to your organization, one that carries significant value well beyond any specific event. It also positions you to be taken seriously and be invited to have a seat at the table. Identifying, articulating, and providing insight into these issues has the potential to change corporate culture, reduce absenteeism and turnover, lower hiring costs, build morale, create better customer service, and even increase revenues.

So how should you proceed? Let's look at what we know about sales people and what you'll need to find out. Top performers typically know what works for them, what doesn't, what they'd like to see more of, and what they suggest other team members need to be as successful. If they have a highly successful regional or functional manager in common, you might consider tapping this person as a trainer at the next sales meeting. Top performers may have a specific habit worth highlighting. How can you capture that? Businesses grow when they can identify what works for their top performers, find ways to replicate it, and teach it to others.

Mid-level performers, who typically comprise the largest segment of a sales team, have the greatest potential for creating an impact if you can motivate and inspire them to up their performance. They should be treated like any other audience: you must identify and address *their* pain points if you want to understand how to effectively reach them and teach them. What do they need more of to close more deals? What gets in their way? To what do they attribute their success and how can they replicate it more often? What support, tools, and information do they need to boost their numbers?

Feedback from low-level performers is also invaluable. Again, yours is a fact-finding mission. What isn't working for them and why? Were they hired after the last sales event and are, therefore, lacking knowledge? Did the same person hire all the low performers thus pointing to a potential error in hiring judgment that needs to be addressed? Do they need a separate track at the event to get more product knowledge, reinforce the brand's messaging, role play, etc.? Most people don't like being at the back of the pack. Offering an opportunity to help them achieve greater success is usually met with enthusiasm and a new degree of trust and openness. (And, yes, you may have to endure some whining and complaining, too.)

Compile and share the Data Discovery results with the Master Strategy Team. The information you've gathered will shape the upcoming meeting's content. Here's what Jack found out.

Jack reached out to a cross-section of the sales team to hear their perspectives and discover why they think sales are lagging. He learns that the company is losing sales to competitors who house their inventory locally and don't have to rely on trucking the equipment in for shows. Castle House hasn't been sufficiently prepared to pivot when an onsite need arises that requires a different equipment configuration. To add to the problem, trucks often break down in transit, so gear arrives later than scheduled. The result is frustrated customers who are prompted to look elsewhere.

Jack's proactive calls with the sales team also uncovered a need for real-time inventory tracking. Although important, addressing that challenge with software doesn't solve the immediate issue of customers needing faster access to equipment. The team needs to know where available equipment is locally and have reliable trucks to pick it up and deliver it on time.

Armed with this critical information, Jack called together the Strategic Vision Team and shared his findings. There was some initial surprise and head scratching. This wasn't what they expected to hear. But then they set to work to devise a new plan. With almost a full year's lead time before the next annual sales meeting, there was plenty of time to explore the necessary changes and have them ready to launch.

The event content would focus on the new initiatives to improve reliability and delivery times by switching to an express freight delivery carrier and ensuring that storage spaces in key locations would house the most in-demand equipment locally. The sales team was excited; they felt validated. Clients would now get what they expected, which would reduce turnover. More inventory would mean an opportunity to increase not just sales, but also customer satisfaction and loyalty, company morale, and sales commissions! The operations team determined that they could outsource trucking and storage rental for less than it would cost to develop, implement, and train the team on new inventory management software. This time, the event was a success from all perspectives and it supported two of the three goals in the vision plan.

Adopting a strategic approach resulted in a great set of solutions that created wins inside and outside the organization. There just may be something to this....

"Until we better understand attendees' needs we wont know if the event's content is adequate."

~ CHRISTY LAMAGNA

CHAPTER SIX

Measuring What Matters

"Knowledge is Power."

~FRANCIS BACON

Key Terms for This Chapter:

- ✦ Return on Investment (ROI)
- ✦ M.I.C.E
- ✦ Meeting Objective
- ✦ Qualitative
- ✦ Quantitative
- ✦ Audits
- ✦ Ecosystem
- ✦ Corporate Social Responsibility (CSR)
- ✦ Strategic Meetings

Many of us are familiar with the phrase **Return on Investment (ROI)**, but few of us truly know what that entails. It's a squishy concept we acknowledge but are not sure how to approach. According to John Nawn, founder of The Perfect Meeting, Inc., understanding metrics requires a better understanding of data in general and how you harness it.

The Ubiquitous Nature of Data

2,500,000,000,000,000,000 or 2.5 quintillion. That's the number of bytes of *new* data that are generated worldwide every day, according to DOMO, a cloud-based business intelligence and analytics platform. To call it a tsunami is a gross understatement.

Humans are largely responsible for generating the bulk of this data, but machine-generated data (industrial equipment, vehicles, medical devices, search engines, sensors, security cameras, etc.) are catching up fast.

✧ Among the most aggressive industries striving to capitalize on data are:

- Finance
- Agriculture
- Education
- Transportation
- Healthcare
- Communications
- Manufacturing
- Energy

As a result, businesses of all shapes and sizes are rapidly transforming themselves and their business strategies to take competitive advantage of all this data.

New disciplines like analytics, artificial intelligence, data mining, machine learning, and predictive modeling allow new ways to aggregate, analyze, and visualize data. The actions taken as a result of the data may be made by human or machine. New professions like data scientist, data architect, and econometrician (who use statistical tools to test economic theories and relationships), are emerging to capitalize on this phenomenon.

M.I.C.E., or the Meetings, Incentives, Conferences, and Exhibitions industry, isn't known for being particularly data-driven. But like every other industry, we're generating more and more data every day and recognizing the need to harness and understand it. And like every other profession, the job security of meeting professionals will depend on our ability to apply the data to design more effective and efficient meetings and events.

Every meeting owner and the professionals who are producing it need to keep the purpose of the meeting in mind. In other words, answering the key question, "Will this event create business value?"

The challenge with a logistics-based model, he observes, is that no one, neither meeting owners nor meeting professionals, can say with any certainty that the results they're getting for their investment in time and money is meeting the business' objective. This is largely because no one working on the event has been privy or asked what they are. But given the significant resources organizations dedicate to meetings and events, they can no longer afford to ignore the question of business value. To do so is fiscally irresponsible, especially when the solution is simply waiting to be applied.

Much has been written about the disruptive nature of technology, but for the meetings industry, the discussion has mostly focused on how it's changing the *way* we meet. The real disruption will come as a result of all the data generated by new technologies, and the impact will be felt in a number of ways. The first might be whether a face-to-face meeting should be held at all. But since humans are social creatures, more likely it will manifest in our ability to craft personalized vehicles for exchanging information in ways we can only dream about now.

Measure What Matters

As Peter Drucker, the father of modern management, put it, "If you can't measure it, you can't improve it."

Historically, meetings and events have been perceived as tied to the cost of doing business. The primary focus on logistics meant that we didn't know to consider inputs and outputs from a broad range of business stakeholders or consider the event's business value. Our post-event evaluations have been little more than performance reviews for meeting professionals. They confirmed if the logistical bases were covered to everyone's satisfaction (registration, transportation, housing, food and beverage, etc.). These evals rarely touched on whether the attendees, exhibitors, or sponsors got significant value from physically coming together. Did they get value hearing what they heard, seeing what they saw, having the time and space to absorb new ideas and imagine new possibilities for themselves and their business?

Measurement is the first step toward improving individual and organizational event outcomes, as well as evaluating indicators that establish professional respect and credibility for those who manage these events. Our lack of insight and understanding of metrics and the data it generates represents a real barrier to more effective decision support, increased credibility, and greater organizational recognition.

So, how do you start measuring what matters? Backward. You start by asking the organization leaders the simple question, "What are your goals and objectives?"

This is the key question that differentiates the perspectives of traditional planners with event strategists.

Traditional planners begin with questions that focus primarily on logistics:

> "When would you like to hold a meeting?"

> "How many people are you expecting?"

> "What location did you have in mind?"

While these questions are important, these details should come later, after you determine the business value of your meeting or event. The only way to determine value is to ask about the business goals and meeting objectives. For clarification, business goals are the observable end results that are critical to the company's success. Examples include: new business development, increased market share, reduced safety incidents, streamlined supply chain, etc. Goals typically have a set of objectives that further detail the nature of the goal.

A **meeting objective** is a specific and measurable targeted outcome that is tied to a particular business goal. Examples might include a 5% increase in the customer base, 10% fewer quality control cases, 25% faster product deliveries to the channel etc.

Few event industry professionals pay attention to information at this level. But to earn respect from executives, it's imperative to translate business goals into strategic meetings and events and then translate the **qualitative** and **quantitative** metrics you can collect, analyze, interpret, report and act on back into the business language the C-suite speaks: increased revenues, reduced costs, greater mind, and market share, etc.

I'm not saying that event producers never think strategically, but in smaller companies or companies where non-professionals step in to develop meetings and events, this limited thinking has been the prevailing approach. It's placed a severe limitation on the perceived value of our industry and its inclusion in broader strategic planning activities.

Quantitative data is sometimes referred to as "hard" data, while qualitative data is often called "soft" data. Here are some examples.

Examples of Hard and Soft Data

Hard Data	Soft Data
Sales	Satisfaction
Units produced	Engagement
New accounts	Innovation
Meeting costs	Awareness

For those of us who believe anything is measurable, there's no limit to the number of metrics you can collect. The key is selecting the *right* metrics.

Hard data may not be available in some industries and can be a lagging indicator of business conditions, so soft data is then often used as a supplement. Soft data, however, are harder to convert into monetary values.

For the most part, the *right* metrics vary from business to business and meeting to meeting. The important thing to do is start at the end and work backward. I recommend that you determine if a metric provides actionable information for your event or more broadly for the business. Ask yourself this question each time you add a new category for measurement and a way of gathering that data. Focus on whether the metric offers a better understanding of the business value of your meeting or event.

Behavioral shifts are harder to measure than, say, more attendees than last year or whether the event met its budget and sponsorship goals. But there are ways of tracking these shifts. Let's break it down by category and review the questions you should ask of attendees to gather this insight.

Content and training effectiveness:

- What percentage of the information presented can you implement immediately?
- Did you leave with knowledge or a new skill you need to do your job better? If so, please provide an example.
- How likely are you to do something in a new way as a result of what you learned? Please explain and quantify.

Business results:

- How likely are these new skills and knowledge to bring you closer to your performance goals?
- What aspect of your job will show the greatest improvement as you apply your new skills and knowledge?
- Did you forge or strengthen relationships that will enhance or extend your effectiveness?

Effectiveness of support tools:

- Were you given the tools you needed to implement new skills?
- How likely is your manager to support you in using your new skills and tools?

Instructor effectiveness:

- Did the session description match the content presented?
- From your perspective, what do you see as the presenter's goal in creating the content?

Follow-up suggestions and needs:

- What additional information or resources do you need to maximize the value of your new skills, knowledge, or relationships?

- What would you change about the event content, format, breakouts, or networking sessions that would make them more helpful to you?

Audits

Traditionally, planners send out post-show surveys that gather information about the event's logistics: general session content quality on a scale of 1 to 10, quality of speakers, quality of meals, etc. And often the gathered information is forgotten or buried somewhere when it's time to start planning for the following year's event. Even if it is available, it isn't relevant when determining the WHY or necessarily the effectiveness of having achieved it. The good news is, except for the time spent, they're free.

Strategists, too, gather essential feedback, but also hire professionals to conduct audits. **Audits** draw on a wide array of data collection methods including direct observation of the target audience, group and individual interviews, design excursions with key stakeholders, qualitative and quantitative analyses of survey data and more. This is the information that helps influence decisions, drives content development, and achieves goals.

Going from traditional, free surveys to hiring a professional for a full-blown audit is often neither necessary nor feasible. Exploring what pieces of the data collection process would serve your organization best sets the stage for gathering the right data on which to make both event-related and business-level decisions. This is critical as your Strategic Plan matures and demonstrates its worth. Once meetings start moving the needle, upper management begins to embrace the process and rely on the additional data points and insights as keys to further growth. Until then, you can be satisfied with incremental steps in the right direction.

When an audit *is* warranted, strategists can partner with a variety of experts to conduct them. The Perfect Meeting Inc. was kind enough to share its methodology.

The Audit Process

Auditors use multidisciplinary tools and techniques to assess the meeting, event, or tradeshow experience in several relevant areas:

- **Authenticity:** Is the meeting experience aligned with the organization's identity?

- **Community:** Does the meeting foster stronger social connections among attendees?

- **Learning:** Does the meeting balance formal learning (educational sessions) with informal learning (networking activities)?

- **Engagement:** Does the meeting foster stronger *emotional* connections among attendees?

- **Environment:**
    - To what degree does the venue support the meeting's goals and objectives?
    - To what degree does the surrounding **ecosystem** support the goals and objectives of the meeting?
    - Did all meeting elements (logistics) enhance attendees' experience?

The audit should result in a list of specific recommendations to guide meeting stakeholders in planning and executing their next event. The audit is designed to increase the meeting's value for all stakeholder groups.

The Devil Really is in the Details

Now, let's take a closer look at logistics. A brilliant strategic vision can get lost in the chaos if event logistics aren't managed expertly. You'll also measure the ROI for logistics-related costs. Most surveys gather some of the following information:

- Number of attendees (primarily relevant for external audiences)
- Sponsorship revenue
- Early-bird registrations
- Hotel block use
- Negotiated cost savings
- Attrition rates
- Attendance differences due to ancillary "pay-to-play" events
- Press mentions / Share of voice
- Analyst activities
- Change in session engagement from previous event/year
- Change in app engagement from previous event/year
- Change in onsite travel charges and related expenses from previous event/year
- Dollars or items donated for **corporate social responsibility (CSR)** project (backpacks, thumb drives, scholarships, etc.)

Measuring ROI

John Nawn extends his generosity to us yet again by sharing his formula to measure ROI for sessions and educational programs. His *Smart Evaluation* template is in the Strategic Resource Library. John's approach assesses such relevant, trackable variables as learning objectives, instructor effectiveness, content formats, and job performances. Once you begin measuring ROI this way, you will be armed with the very data you need to demonstrate precisely why **strategic meetings** are the *most* effective marketing and sales tool there are.

"Measurement is the first step toward improving individual and organizational event outcomes."

~ JOHN NAWN

CHAPTER SEVEN

What Makes People Tick?

"What have you done for me lately?"

~JANET JACKSON

Key Terms for This Chapter:

✧ WIIFM

✧ Strategic Planner

✧ Engagement Questions

✧ Exploration Questions

✧ Exit Questions

✧ Open-ended Questions

A Peek Inside Human Behavior

Strategists who understand a bit about the psychology of human behavior can often create more effective meeting environments. For our purposes, let's boil this down to three essential principles:

Principle 1: We are *all* motivated by the answer to the question, "What's in it for ME?" (even Mother Theresa)

Principle 2: People's favorite subject is themselves.

Principle 3: When motivating others, it cannot be about you.

Principle 1: What's in it for ME?

The answer to this question drives all human behavior. Here it is useful to think about what are you offering your attendees that is more compelling than any other option they have for that same time block?

Knowing how to answer this question for your target audience is the essence of effective marketing. This is especially important for external audiences, particularly if ticket sales underwrite your event's expenses.

I try to approach every interaction with the thought that I must be the answer to the other person's "What's in it for ME?" (**WIIFM**). This strategy helped me build a multi-million-dollar business, be featured in magazines and national advertising campaigns, and open doors I never imagined would swing wide for me. Knowing how to use WIIFM to your advantage is one of the most powerful lessons you can learn. It applies well beyond event marketing to *every interaction you will have professionally and personally.*

Skeptical that it all comes down to this one simple question? Yep. Humans really are that simple. If you look at your own actions, you'll see that each can all be traced back to WIIFM. Every single one. That doesn't make you selfish, it makes you human. Even the Dali Lama lives by this principle, and, by all accounts, he's a pretty selfless guy. You can be altruistic and simultaneously be governed by WIIFM. Consider this example:

> *Charles and Maggie had been friends since college. Charles had always been famous for finding the perfect gift for his family and friends for any occasion. So, when Maggie found a painting at a small gallery—an expensive painting—by an artist Charles collected, she bought it immediately. She knew he would love it! This also meant she was picking the perfect gift...and she was going to beat him at his own game!*

Aha, WIIFM!

WIIFM also comes into play, perhaps more subtly when you choose to do something that you really don't want to do.

A few months ago, I was returning home after a week of heavy travel and back-to-back speaking engagements, I landed at the Newark airport. It was 4 o'clock on a Friday afternoon and I was beat. On the ride home, I was fantasizing about putting on sweats, pouring a glass of wine, cuddling my dog and binge watching my favorite, yet neglected TV series. It was going to be glorious... My cell phone rang. The caller's name glowed in the dimness of the car's back seat. It was a dear friend who was going through a rough divorce. <Sigh> I answered. Was I in town? Could we meet for an early dinner? She needed to talk. Poof! There went the fantasy. I told her I was on my way.

So where was the WIIFM here? Yes. I desperately wanted to get home and decompress. But my friendships are important to me and have been my salvation in plenty of situations in the past and will be in the future. That requires an investment. So here was a chance to make an investment in my own future. Bam! WIIFM.

Let's bring this back to target audiences. Being able to offer the best answer to WIIFM is the key to driving attendance and producing outcomes. Simply getting bodies in a room isn't your goal. Engaging attendees who are then motivated to behave in a way that supports the company's desired results is. Being the bearer of WIIFM for your audience must be at the forefront of your mind as you create every element of the event experience. That's part of what distinguishes an event planner from a **strategic planner**: the execution of logistics in a way that relieves an audience's pain points, and the creation of content that meets their needs. In doing so, the audience becomes an integral part of your team in helping you attain the events' specific goals...your WIIFM.

This concept of being the best answer to WIIFM applies to both internal and external audiences, but there are subtle differences in the application. Let's start with the similarities.

People are drawn to events for two reasons: meaningful content and networking opportunities. For some, meaningful content may be learning the latest trends in soybean farming. It doesn't matter what the topic; the need for relevant content is universal.

Networking doesn't have to be about exchanging business cards and setting up a new acquaintance for a big business transaction. If you're a huge fan of the show, The Walking Dead, perhaps networking is attending a "Walker Stalker" conference, taking a picture with cast members, and meeting like-minded fanatics. Although much of this book speaks to corporate events and sales teams, it's important to realize that the philosophy behind strategic planning translates to any event and every audience.

Principle 2: People's Favorite Subject is Themselves

Most people love to talk about themselves—even if they seem humble and self-effacing. Nevertheless, each person is at the center of his or her own stories. This may prove tiresome to encounter in your personal life, but it's extraordinarily useful in learning exactly what your target audience thinks, wants and needs… right from the proverbial horse's mouth. Soliciting people's opinions not only gives you the information you need, but it also gives them a sense of validation that they are important to you, which they are, and increases future engagement and loyalty.

Digging into Data

Data gathering is a science and should be managed by someone knowledgeable about the process. As you segue into strategic planning, you may have to wear multiple hats, but eventually, the Data Discovery process should be managed by a contracted professional or a qualified person in your office. Since you or someone on your team may have to roll up your sleeves and take this on, I'll share some background on how to approach Data Discovery.

The value of the information you can gather is contingent on the nature and format of the questions you ask. Remember the technology adage, "garbage in, garbage out?" Make sure you are asking questions if you want to elicit the right information at the right detail level. For instance, "What do you think we should change about the company?" is not likely going to get you the detailed information you can apply to creating content. "What tools do you need to do your job more efficiently?" will. Be ready with a set of ground rules, a list of questions, and an understanding of how to solicit feedback effectively.

Sampling a cross-section of your target audience is the ideal way to get a clear snapshot. It's useful to first establish that each person's input is important and that the event is designed to serve their needs and make them more successful. That sets the tone for an open dialogue. This does not mean everything you hear is objectively true, and unbiased. In fact, very little is objectively true and unbiased, everyone sees information through their own personal lens. What we can do is filter the information for its applicable value.

✧ Suggested Ground Rules for Gathering Feedback:

1. Set the Intention:

    • Lay the foundation for the conversation by sending an email in advance that explains the purpose of your call.

    • Make it clear that your intention is to gather information to create more effective content for the next meeting.

    • Include a few sample questions, so they have a sense of what's coming and can be thinking of responses.

2. Schedule adequate time:

    • When you schedule time for making interview calls, allow more time for yourself to prepare than you expect each call to take. For example, I set aside a four-hour block for multiple calls, so I can focus exclusively on connecting with interviewees and keep the momentum going. I find it difficult to sandwich these kinds of calls between other tasks.

    • For the call itself, schedule enough time to cover the topics, but not so much that participants are leery of carving out an excessive block in their schedules. You don't want to rush the discussion nor do you want to overbook their time.

    • Be prepared. Begin on time to build trust and end on time so you demonstrate integrity and also that you don't keep the next respondent waiting.

3. Decide to attribute or share feedback anonymously

    • It's a good idea to establish a policy on anonymity before calls or ask participants their preference and honor it. Sometimes knowing who said something helps to clarify the context and perhaps any politics behind what was said. Conversely, if people are commenting on an internal event and think their words will be evaluated by their executive team, they may be less candid in their responses, which compromises the value of the information.

- Confirm again with the interviewee whether you can attribute the feedback to them or if they prefer it to be shared anonymously. People are usually eager to share their opinions but not always eager to have their names attributed in case there could be fallout.

- It's up to you and the key stakeholders to determine the goal of the calls and how to best reflect that in policies and approach.

4. You're important to the conversation, but it's not about you.

- Avoid adding your opinion, even subtly. The goal is to gather authentic feedback. People will often change their answers to please the other person. Remain neutral in responding to what they say to avoid unintentionally skewing feedback.

- Just offer the minimal amount of response that lets them know the call hasn't been disconnected.

- Lulls in conversation can make us uncomfortable, so we often try to fill them. Don't do it. Remember that silence is often a reflection of someone thinking, so let it unfold. What is left unsaid by the interviewee carries significance.

- Resist the urge to respond to criticisms, to defend past program elements, or address any specific issues that arose. Even if you know why something had to unfold a particular way, avoid the urge to explain or defend past events.

- Be ready to hear things you won't like; that's the whole point. You *will* hear negative comments, that's where the lessons are. You don't learn much from, "Gosh, everything was swell!"

5. Creating a win-win

- Simply asking people for their opinions makes them feel validated and strengthens relationships.

- Acknowledge their comments and thank them for sharing their opinions with you.

- If they've made suggestions, you can say that you will pass them along, but, of course not all ideas can be implemented. Thank them again for understanding and participating.

What to Ask and How

We've already discussed how uncovering your audience's pain points draws a treasure map to relevant content. Data Discovery begins the process, but how do you dig a little deeper to uncover that treasure?

Rules of Thumb for Crafting Questions

I tapped the Center for Innovation in Research and Teaching, an organization of focus group facilitators, experts in the art of information gathering, for their best practices in crafting and delivering focus groups. While what we're doing isn't exactly the same as a focus group, I find the advice still applies. Here's what they suggest:

You can group the questions based on their role in the discussion. The three types below each guide the discussion to initiate, enrich, and complete the engagement. (I like to think of it like the parts of dance routine or a piece of music).

Engagement questions introduce the participant and interviewee to each other, the topics or subjects at hand, and gets them comfortable enough to start a conversation. As an example, you could start off with something personal. "How's the weather been in [insert the name of their city] the past few weeks?" You can mention how the weather has been where you are. You can then turn to how the weather was during the event they just attended, good or bad, as the basis for a shared experience.

Exploration questions are designed to get into the discussion and touch on the heart of the relevant topics. For instance, you mentioned that you left the event after Day 2: Could you elaborate on why and what might have encouraged you to stay through until the final keynote on Day 3?

Exit questions are designed to capture any angles missed during the discussion or any final suggestions or sentiments. For example: Is there anything else you would like to share about what (insert event name) can provide to help you be more successful?

Open-ended questions are, of course, the gateway to rich conversations. Asking questions that allow for creative feedback, regardless of the feasibility of implementing their suggestions, not only lets your audience know you're open to new ideas, it may actually lead to solutions you hadn't thought of.

✧ Sample Open Ended Item Questions Are:

- What is the single most important thing you would like to learn that would help you do your job more effectively/successfully?

- What do you perceive to be your customers' greatest or most common challenge?

- What is the most important thing you learned last year, at last year's sales meeting (for example) and have you put it into practice?

Once you get each answer, you can make clarifying statements to acknowledge and confirm what you heard them say: "So, to be clear, if you were in charge of this year's event, you would focus the content on more product training and possibly a refresher on how to use the new sales software. Is that right? That's very helpful. Thank you." If you need additional details, you can always ask deeper questions. Watch the clock though, you don't want the interview to become tedious.

A comprehensive list of the Center's questions, some of which I adapted for Data Discovery sessions, is available in the Strategic Resource Library.

Final Steps of the Interview

Get agreement from each interviewee for follow-up calls, emails, or questions. You will likely have additional questions for them or clarifications after the initial conversation, especially as you master this process. Again, be mindful of the interviewees' time and keep follow ups short and to the point. They may also have questions or concerns about what they've said. Invite them to contact you if they do.

After the Interview

Within 24 hours of the interview, follow up with a Thank You email indicating your appreciation of their time and their input and how it will help make events better in the future. (Of course, hand-written thank-you notes are a nice touch if you have their addresses and the time). Decide who should send out the email: a company executive, you, perhaps the person on your team who conducted the interview. Determine which option sets the right tone: a balance of respect, gratitude, and friendliness. Alternatively, you can set up an email alias (event-team@mycompany.com), for instance, if you want responses back to the email to go to multiple people, or you specifically want to hide individuals' email addresses—but this approach is a bit cooler in tone. If you agreed to treat feedback anonymously, reinforce that in the note (and make sure that happens).

Principle 3: (Once again,) It's not about you

There is a fine line between your professional and personal expertise. You get paid for your expertise. You are usually not a representative of your target audience, so your opinions aren't always relevant.

Here's a classic example of a planner allowing an opinion to get in the way of a professional decision.

Karin was a mid-level executive at a legal firm whose colleagues were predominantly men. The dress code was formal and so was the atmosphere in their New York City office with dark wood and masculine artwork. For six months of the year, Karin was tasked with planning the firm's annual meeting and hired an SME to assist. She followed our lead with the strategic initiatives and most of the details, but when it came to décor, Karin wanted to take the lead.

Unbeknownst to us, Karin was a frustrated wedding planner. Capitalizing on the firm's generous budget, Karin spent countless hours working with the very expensive designer florist. She was obsessed. She wanted expansive sprays of colorful flowers in huge crystal vases and she wanted them everywhere. Our lead strategist discovered Karin's proclivities and pointed out that elaborate florals didn't fit with the event's rather austere and conservative audience. Karin was unswerving. On the day of the event, the firm's partners and clients seemed a bit confused when they entered the meeting space. Fortunately, the flowers only made a few of them sneeze, and most barely noticed once the event got started.

While the florals didn't impede the event's purpose, they were a tremendous waste of money and were not in synch with the rest of the event. When in doubt, return to the goals, the target-audience feedback, and the historical data for grounding. Keep a few attendees you know well on speed dial to get candid feedback. *Your* opinion shouldn't enter the equation unless you represent the target audience (and chances are you don't). All steps in the Discovery Process-and any deeper research you do, will be critical for the optimal success of the event. Armed with a clearer understanding of what your audience wants, let's you give your presenters the insight and direction they need to begin creating the right content and delivery.

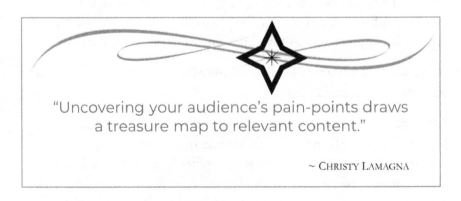

"Uncovering your audience's pain-points draws a treasure map to relevant content."

~ CHRISTY LAMAGNA

CHAPTER EIGHT

Learning, Mindfulness, and Inclusion

"You can change your world by changing your words."

~JOEL OSTEEN

Key Terms for This Chapter:

✧ Learning Environment

✧ Passive Learning

✧ Active Learning / The Socratic Method

✧ Mindfulness

✧ Mindful Meetings

✧ Meeting Planning

Strategic events bring relevance and meaning not only to *what* content is presented, but also to *how* and *where* it's presented. We refer to this as the **learning environment**. Meetings are slowly moving away from the long-standing and predictable pattern of breakfast for an hour, followed by the general session, a morning break, back to the ballroom, lunch, more general session, pm break, and back to the ballroom. Yawn.

Each time attendees are shepherded into a ballroom, the lights go down and a seemingly endless parade of speakers takes the stage. The process consumes about eight hours and rarely results in people dancing in the aisles or spontaneously yelling "HALLELUJAH!" during a presentation. Hardly. Yet, we continue to host meetings this way.

Anyone who has attended a conference with this format knows that "death by PowerPoint" is possible. Add the carbohydrate-laden breakfasts and lunches, and you have the perfect recipe for a very expensive snooze fest.

✧ For an event to truly inspire learning and carry value, it must:

- Be meaningful to the audience
- Offer information presented by a qualified (and hopefully, engaging) speaker
- Reinforce concepts through repetition (without being patronizing)
- Include opportunities for comments and questions
- Acknowledge, encourage, and praise individuals and the audience as a whole for their contributions and achievements

Do I Really Have to Sit Through This?

For event sessions to be effective, content must resonate with attendees, and cannot be presented in a "one-size-fits-all" manner. Studies show that attendees who are offered the option to design their own onsite learning experience reportedly enjoy a higher level of learning and retention than those who participate in mandatory and predetermined group sessions. Keynotes, general sessions, and morning kickoffs should be launch pads for custom breakouts and other focused, more intimate activities.

Offering concurrent breakout sessions does require more space and tighter logistics management, but it allows your attendees access to more content choices over the same time period and allows them to customize their curriculum. Everything hinges, though, on the assembly and delivery of quality content. This is where most of your energy should be focused. Everything else; décor, menus, accommodations, is secondary. The less appealing it sounds to focus on content curation, the greater the likelihood is that your events need attention in this area.

Paving the Road to Success

Data Discovery results hold the keys to what breakouts should be offered. During those conversations, your audience identified their pain points and needs. Those issues must be addressed before behaviors can change. When obstacles are removed, goals are easier to reach. Your content needs to provide information, training, inspiration, and motivation for new behaviors to take shape and success to be achieved.

Every speaker, facilitator, breakout moderator, and panelist should have received the portion of the Event Objectives Calendar pertaining to the meeting currently being planned. They must understand how their presentation or participation aids in achieving the stated goals. They must also understand who the audience is and the expected learning outcomes at the end of each session.

When considering who should lead breakouts or be asked to speak, start by looking within your organization. Look past the key executives who are expected to speak and find the people who are subject matter experts, role models, record setters, overachievers and the subject of success stories. Giving someone within the organization a formal opportunity to inspire and teach others validates their efforts and may prove more effective than relying solely on top-level or outside presenters. There is value in seeing "one of your own" in front of a room. Having someone who knows not just the mechanics of how to succeed but who understands the organization's culture brings a level of intimacy and familiarity to the process. (Chapter 24 discusses how to prepare and train those who are not professional speakers to effectively present to an audience.)

When your actions are mindfully centered on a specific goal, the logistics begin to flow naturally. Suddenly pieces easily fall into place, creating momentum and clarity. One good decision facilitates the next, creating an intentional cohesion that is completely synchronous. Costs often go down, results improve, and the process becomes easier than it's ever been. When everyone is on the same page, it creates an energy that propels the process forward. Fewer mistakes are made because decisions take place in a defined context. Extraneous spend is eliminated and dollars are allocated where they are needed most. You often find you have money for things you never could have afforded before.

One is the Loneliest Number

We are creatures of habit. When we walk into a meeting room, most of us look for a similarly located seat every time. We settle in, listen to the presenter if what is being said resonates, sneak in a few glances at those sitting around us, perhaps jot down a few notes, even ask a question if we're feeling particularly engaged and then head to the next session.

Listening to a presenter and taking notes is called **passive learning**. Adult learners tend to learn better when they participate and interact with the instructor and with other participants. This is called **active learning**. It is also referred to as **the Socratic Method**, named after the Greek philosopher, Socrates, who taught students by asking question after question. Allowing participants to draw from their own experience, interact in groups and solve problems produces a better learning outcome. We are better able to internalize new ideas when we are engaged. Active learning may not work in every context, the CEO's welcome address or the CFO's financial forecast, for instance, but it should be considered as an option whenever appropriate.

Take a Seat

Theater and classroom configurations have been the "go to" room sets, and although they have served several purposes well, more creative options are beginning to supplant them. Setups where attendees face each other can encourage interactivity and learning by fostering conversation. This can help attendees absorb content better, which means achieving your desired behavioral changes faster. Remember, the reason we meet is to achieve goals. Content and engagement leads us there.

Not sure where to start with creative room designs? I've provided some room set options and a description of what type of experience they support in the Strategic Resource Library, which includes a comprehensive reference file provided by Paul Collins from Jordan-Webb.

Different people process information in different ways and at different speeds. Some need more time than others to absorb and process information. Packing the schedule with back-to-back sessions doesn't ensure more learning. Some people may simply reach a saturation point where they can no longer take in more information until they've had some time to digest the most recent input. Often, factual information delivered in a graphical format can help people to grasp and process new ideas more effectively. In other words, data speaks louder than words. In fact, here's some data to back that up.

According to University of Illinois psychology professor Alejandro Llerashi, prolonged attention to a single task *hinders* performance. Llerashi proposes deactivating and reactivating your goals allows you to stay focused. "From a practical standpoint," said Llerashi, "our research suggests that, when faced with long tasks (such as studying before a final exam or doing your taxes), it is best to impose brief breaks on yourself. Brief mental breaks will actually help you stay focused on your task!"

A study by *The Muse* provides insight into what is ideal timing for encouraging productivity and learning: "Specifically, the most productive people work for 52 minutes at a time, then break for 17 minutes before getting back to it."

Our challenge is always to find a balance between including in an event the necessary content and allocating enough time for it all to happen, and also factoring in sufficient "white space," or breaks, for people to be able to absorb it all and reap the benefits. That can be tricky. Asking presenters to leave 15 minutes at the end of their session for participants to discuss, reflect, and digest what they have just heard sounds good in theory, but rarely plays out that way. Speakers keep talking, phones come out, people get antsy and the moment is lost.

If you want an audience to remember, the speaker should be focused so the audience can focus; less rambling equals more retention.

Mindfulness in Meetings

The way to center attention is through **mindfulness. Mindful meetings** reflect a culture of learning, focusing attention on what is happening in the moment. Text messages, endless emails, and external calls tug at an audience's attention. Strategies to keep an audience in the moment is part of the ongoing evolution of the strategic event blueprint. Creating purposeful goal-achieving content provides a head start when creating a culture of meeting mindfulness. But then one has to find ways to keep the audience coming back to the here and now, often through opportunities for interactivity.

Holly Duckworth, an expert on mindful meetings as well as an event professional, brings mindfulness to event strategy. She illustrates how strategists can incorporate the practice into events and meetings to keep the audience's attention on the present. Below is an excerpt from an article Holly wrote for the Spring 2018 issue of *Midwest Meetings*, entitled, "*Mindfulness can be as simple as ABC—Affirmations, Breathing, and Centering.*" She describes these three practices as follows:

Affirmations – Our words are the most powerful thing we have in our world. They literally shape the thoughts, feelings, and experiences we have. If you say, "I'm so busy, I'm so busy," you create, attract, and magnetize "busier" to you. Don't want busier? Write an affirmation of its opposite. Affirmations are short sentences that create the positive reality you wish to have. For example, "I am centered in my work knowing my work is easy and makes the world a better place." Say this affirmation multiple times each day and post it in your car or office to remind you.

Breathing – It is the very essence of our life, and yet we take for granted the next breath will be there. Breathing returns our focus to life. Do it now; take a second to feel the air coming in your nose and out your mouth. Remember the life that moves through you does it easefully and so should your work be easeful. Even three focused breaths three times a day can reduce your stress.

Centering – Centering is practicing the process of reconnecting to the still, small voice inside of you. Move your awareness from your brain doing-ness to your heart of being-ness. Centering in partnership with breathing can give you the few moments of necessary calm and recovery needed amidst the demands of the **meeting planning** profession today. It's also the chance to listen to what your heart wants you to know.

Holly notes that as you work with the ABC technique, look for places where you can have meeting participants create affirmations for the meeting or take a moment to breathe and center before a keynote or breakout sessions. These three mindfulness practices will result in people being more peaceful, present, productive and, over time, more profitable.

Ironically, those who would benefit most from mindfulness often discount its value. If you're one of these people, over-scheduled, exhausted and stressed, I invite you to think about this: If practicing mindfulness can bring some sanity and focus to your out of control life, as it has for so many, couldn't you set aside a few minutes to see if it works for you? If it doesn't work, you're no worse off. It can take as little as 10 minutes a day and chances are, if you make an honest attempt, you will be pleasantly surprised.

One Size Does Not Fit All (Ages)

Your organization's audience profile may span multiple generations. Acknowledging that there are differences between how each generation learns, communicates, processes, and shares information is an integral part of creating a diverse and inclusive environment that fosters participation and learning.

Below is a compilation of some online research results about various generations in today's workforce; how they are defined and a few characteristics about their learning styles.

How Generations are Defined

Generation / Birth Years	Attributes	Predominant Learning Style
Matures (1925 - 1945)	Traditionalists in approach, Mature Generation respects hierarchy and authority. Stoic. Communicate indirectly to avoid challenging the existing order.	It is important for this age group to be recognized for their qualifications and experience.
Baby Boomers (1946 - 1964)	Task focused and achievement oriented, Baby Boomers like competitive environments.	They expect a more personally focused learning structure. Prefer in class participation.
Generation X (1965 - 1980)	Impatient and goal orientated, Gen-Xers want to work hard and have the freedom to make their own decisions.	Skeptical and at times challenging, Hungry for knowledge and feedback. They prefer on-the-job learning.
Generation Y (1981 – 1999)	Gen-Yers value development and flexibility. They challenge authority and are less likely to stick to the rules than Gen-Xers or Baby Boomers.	Collaborative. Ready access to technologies, which they see as embedded in everything they do. They favor learning while doing, with regular coaching and feedback.
Generation Z (after 2000, Millennials)	Highly networked and tech-aware. They have a reputation for short attention spans and little patience for traditional attitudes or approaches.	Less information, more evaluation. Want to be engaged by multiple learning channels. Prefer to experience information rather than have it spoon-fed to them.

Something Old, Something New, Something Different, All are True

The way people consume content and experience meetings is evolving. Understanding your audience, their learning styles, preferences and needs enable you to create and present content that passes the "WIIFM" test every time.

Finding the perfect balance between technology-driven communications and "old school" techniques, including paper and now event email (according to Generation Y), probably isn't realistically going to happen—especially if you're communicating with multiple generations. Those who are resistant to technology (Matures) are either going to ignore it or use it begrudgingly (or badly). They may still prefer paper, and you can try to accommodate them (though organizations increasingly have sustainability rules about printing). If you have a lot of Matures in your audience, you could strike a balance by offering a limited number of printed schedules onsite. Then indicate how any updates will be shared: to the event app, to electronic signs or white boards, and/or sent out via text message. By contrast, Gen-Zers often don't even carry a pen or wear a watch (unless it's a smart watch). Their relationships with electronic devices and information are as fundamental as breathing air.

Accommodate as many types as you think are representative of your audience and that you can afford to accommodate. Remember being and feeling included is an integral part of the audience's successful on-site experience.

This also means including those who cannot be onsite. If feasible, consider live streaming the event so those offsite can participate in real time, complete with the ability to post questions to speakers.

Everyone is Welcome

Being attuned to the rich diversity and learning styles of attendees applies to more than generational learning differences. Gender balance is another timely and significant aspect of diversity and inclusion. Look at the speakers and panelists you've brought on. Are they all or mostly all male? Look for qualified women who have established themselves as experts in a particular field and consider creating a balanced speaker roster.

You will also want to pay attention to people with special needs. This is imperative. Focus on accessibility when choosing a location. And remember that some special needs aren't as readily visible, but are nonetheless real. Handicaps might include attention deficit disorder, for instance. So, if an attendee gets up and walks out of a room, hold your judgment. They may just be taking care of themselves.

Doors that open with a handicap-accessible button are helpful to those in wheelchairs and those without the physical strength to pull open a door. You should expect to have to make some accommodations.

In fact, you may want to include a question on the registration form inquiring if a scooter or other accessibility accommodations are needed, particularly if the distance between sleeping rooms and meeting rooms is significant (think any hotel in Las Vegas). If so, you should plan to make the accommodation at the event's expense. *You* chose the space not the attendees, so choose with diversity in mind. Inclusion goes beyond arranging logistics; it's a state of mind.

Consider adding a comprehensive question to your registration to widen your inclusion efforts. Consider: "Tell us what you need to fully participate. Please share any needs, including cognitive, mobility, sight, hearing, chemical sensitivities and other specifics. This will allow attendees to give you the information to be as inclusive as possible.

Once you're onsite, take a moment to stop and look around. Pay attention to the energy, intensity, and the number of conversations happening around you. Events bring people together for a shared experience. They intensify relationships (be that for the better or worse), create memories and provide to those who likely spend much of their day behind a screen a chance to be face to face and three-dimensional— to be seen, heard and hopefully appreciated. It's great to focus on achieving monetary goals, but the relationships and trust built at events are priceless. Your part in making this happen is instrumental.

"Inclusion goes beyond arranging logistics;
it's a state of mind."

~ CHRISTY LAMAGNA

CHAPTER NINE

Keeping the Conversation Going

"Change is the end result of all true learning."

~LEO BUSCAGLIA

Key Terms for This Chapter:

✧ Forgetting Curve

✧ Spaced Repetition Method

✧ External Audience

✧ Internal Audience

✧ Continuous Communication Cycle®

✧ Internal Marketing Program®

✧ Standard Operating Procedures (SOP)

✧ For learning to be optimally effective, messages must:

- Be relevant to the audience and their needs
- Be appropriate in length
- Be presented effectively by an expert in both the topic and in teaching it
- Be reinforced through repetition and the opportunity to ask questions
- Acknowledge, encourage, and praise achievements as they occur

Hearing someone talk about a concept is not the same as learning it.

German psychologist Hermann Ebbinghaus came up with a theory called the **Forgetting Curve**. It refers to what happens in the period just after learning has taken place when we start to forget what we have just learned. According to his findings, we tend to forget 50 to 80 percent of all new information within a few days after the learning event has occurred. Recall improves significantly when the learning is spaced out over time and repeated during the teaching session. Long-term retention using this **spaced repetition method**, improves by as much as 200 percent.

Data to the Rescue Once Again

To be effective, onsite education should be part of a continuous, strategic communication plan that reinforces learning, encourages dialogue, and rewards incremental improvements.

Think of how many speakers you've listened to during your events who have inspired you, at the time, to nod your head, take pages of notes, full of underlines and exclamation marks, and got you amped up about the changes you were going to make in your life. Did that happen? Do you even remember what those changes were? Do you know which pile those notes are under...?

One of the reasons you likely didn't make those changes is because you returned to your life and picked up where you left off. The event and the ideas it inspired are no longer top of mind. Don't beat yourself up about it. That was almost guaranteed to happen.

External vs. Internal Marketing Programs

If your event is targeted to an **external audience**, the chances are high that there is already a plan in place to leverage your event content, and keep the conversation going. The importance of repetition and remaining top of mind, as it relates not just to learning but to increasing profits and growing market share, is indisputable. Advertising executives used to follow "The Marketing Rule of Seven" which stated that a message needed to be heard at least seven times before someone would purchase a product or service. That concept was created in 1930. With social media's pervasiveness it takes a lot more than seven attempts to get someone's attention and inspire them to change their behavior.

It may come as no surprise then that, according to Statista, projected marketing spending in just the United States in 2018 will be $457.6 billion. That's a lot of message reinforcement!

But what if your event is targeted to an **internal audience**? Are plans in place to keep that audience engaged and inspire a change in their behavior? Internal audiences, sales teams specifically, need the same reinforcement of ideas and continued engagement to drive desired behavior. Think about it: both audiences need to feel, think, say, and do specific things for an organization to achieve its financial objectives. Why then do we go with a "one-and-done" method with onsite learning? And how is it that people wonder why employee behavior isn't changing?

Creating a **continuous communication cycle**, or **internal marketing program**, will do for your internal audience what your outward-facing marketing efforts do for your clients and prospects. If the goal is to influence behavior across your entire value chain, the *internal* sales team is an obvious place to start.

Your marketing communications team may already have an ongoing dialogue with employees in the form of an e-newsletter, internal company website, etc. Unless your internal event is targeted at the entire organization, the continuous communication cycle I'm suggesting must be an addition to the current messaging. The message needs to be specific to the people whose behavior you are trying to influence, so an employee newsletter's content won't be specific enough to change behavior for the sales team, and messages directed only to the sales team won't be effective in achieving goals if the initiative is company-wide.

If you're seeing dollar signs, exhale. An extensive budget to fund an internal marketing campaign would be wonderful but is not necessary. That said, remember: strategic planning will likely reduce total event costs by creating a potential opportunity that will fund initiatives like this.

Content on Demand

Here are some ways to inexpensively combat the Forgetting Curve and create an internal marketing program.

Keep content accessible by posting it online, if it isn't already, after the conference. If slides were used, post those along with the audio or video recordings of the presentations. If the sessions aren't confidential, consider posting the recordings on your company's YouTube channel. (If your organization permits the use of thumb drives, you may want to offer a promotional opportunity to a sponsor to provide a branded thumb drive to attendees with show content on it, and their pre-approved messaging—though lead time on this may make it more difficult to ensure that the content on the drive reflects last-minute changes.)

If you have the resources to maintain and monitor an online discussion community to continue the conversation and reinforce key content, I highly recommend it to build relationships.

When you are selecting speakers, ask whether they would be willing to contribute a small bit of content each month to keep their message and expertise top of mind with the community. Posting their content to a discussion board, newsletter, etc., provides relevant information from an expert who the participants have already learned from, and it takes the burden of creating fresh content off an internal team. When you look at logistics strategically, negotiating content from a speaker while solidifying the speaking contract is simply common sense. They are likely to do this at no charge to keep their name and services top of mind with the audience also. It's a win-win.

Organizations committed to influencing behavior and accelerating their sales cycles commit to internal marketing programs. As the Master Strategist, it's your job to introduce the concept and the data behind it. Your team won't be doing the work, but it's your responsibility to put the **standard operating procedures (SOPs)** in place and oversee the entire strategic implementation process.

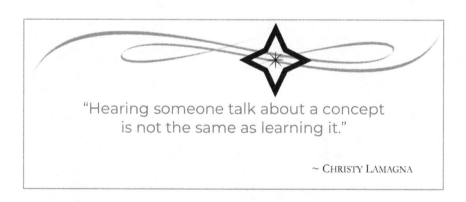

"Hearing someone talk about a concept is not the same as learning it."

~ CHRISTY LAMAGNA

CHAPTER TEN

Designing an Environment for Change

"We are what we repeatedly do. Excellence, then, is not an act, but a habit."

~ARISTOTLE

Key Terms for This Chapter:

- ✧ Experiential Design
- ✧ Environmental Design
- ✧ Meeting Design

In 1887, the famous American philosopher and psychologist William James keenly observed:

> "[In] the acquisition of a new habit, or the leaving of an old one, we must take care to launch ourselves with as strong and decided an initiative as possible. Accumulate all the possible circumstances which shall reinforce the right motives; put yourself assiduously in conditions that encourage the new way; make engagements incompatible with the old; take a public pledge; if the case allows; in short, envelop your resolution with every aid you know. This will give you your new beginning such a momentum that the temptation to break down will not occur as soon as it otherwise might, and every day during which a breakdown is postponed adds to the chances of it not occurring at all."

One can see this idea demonstrated in the meeting industry today through the popular concept of **experiential** or **environmental design**.

Capturing your attendees' attention from your first communication onward is a key principle of **meeting design**.

Events are the only three-dimensional embodiment of marketing messages. Therefore, how the event is designed is the art of bringing those messages to life. For new behaviors to form, event strategists must create an environment that encourages, supports, sets the tone for, and rewards change.

John Nawn defines meeting design as "the purposeful shaping of form and content to achieve desired results." It combines traditional design disciplines (interior design, instructional design, and service design) with emerging design disciplines (experience design, interactivity design, emotional design, sensory design, and environmental design) to meet business and event goals and objectives.

Julian Lwin, spatial innovation and experiential design director of Lwin Designs, describes his job this way:

> "My role can be described as an omni-dimensional storyteller. I take a client's brand narrative and create an immersive 'theater-like experience' by designing the staging, lighting, sound, visual cues and decor."

> "Successful brand experiences offer genuine engagement with those who encounter them. In designing those memorable exchanges, clients must understand the value of empathy. It is this empathy that inspires customers to develop a relationship with a brand, which, in turn, leads to new and repeat business. Banal design experiences, instead, isolate customers and do little to engage and retain them. Strategic and well-conceived designs, on the other hand, have the power to transform events and experiences into sublime happenings with excitement and a tangible buzz."

> "This is what I strive for in my work. It's where true return on investment percolates. Current research indicates that creating engaging customer 'experiences' leads to greater brand loyalty and investment."

"I orchestrate a journey that connects brand initiatives with an audience. For the performance, the leading actors are cars, fashion collections, fragrances, data, technology or new product launches. My role is like that of a theater director— where every detail of a performance is stage-managed to evoke maximum empathy and meaningful, enduring impact."

The Westin provides a prime example of experiential design. Their "For a Better You" program was designed around the guest's entire hotel experience, extending well beyond its traditional well-appointed lobby, guest accommodations, and restaurants.

Westin's signature white-tea scent brings their brand to life from the moment a guest walks through their doors. The sense of smell is closely linked with memory, which may cause a guest to unconsciously associate the scent of the hotel with a happy experience when and where they detected a similar scent. Using effective event design, the Westin's signature scent leaves a deeper impression on guests than an impressive lobby at a fraction of the cost of renovation.

Whenever possible, strive to engage all five senses when creating your meeting environment. As we've mentioned, strategic events are the only three-dimensional embodiment of marketing messages, making them the most powerful marketing tool there is. A-list celebrities get paid millions to showcase cars, watches, and perfume in magazines and on TV, which are only two-dimensional experiences. Strategic events create experiences that influence what people think, say, and do for a fraction of the traditional marketing and advertising cost. Strategic planners drive the vehicle that delivers the most effective and expeditious change agent at a company's disposal.

At this point, you're likely starting to see the parts falling into place. Meeting design supports meeting mindfulness, which supports content, which supports objectives, which support goals. Each piece is related to the other, and each task weaves the pieces together. Note: I used the term woven, not cemented, in place. We all know the key to planning is flexibility! As the adage goes; Man plans, God laughs.

I once attended a sales meeting during which Eminem's "Lose Yourself" played as the walk-on, walk-off, intro *and* walk out music at varying decibels. *For four days.* It was as close to being tortured as I have ever come. The EVP of sales thought it was thematic and inspiring. It wasn't.

We've all been to meetings that have been branded from top to bottom. Someone had a clever idea and ran with it. And ran and ran and ran. As the poet Robert Browning said in his 1855 poem *Andrea del Sarto*, "Less is more." He knew what he was talking about. Overexposure to anything, even awesome things like wine or chocolate chip cookies, can have a negative effect (just ask my hips). That same thing holds true for onsite branding.

When attendees are assaulted with a clever motivational slogan, on signage, in music, on slides, on giveaway items, and at evening parties, they reach saturation and tune it out. Likewise, messages should resonate with attendees. While "Boost Performance," "Kick It Up a Notch," and "Reach New Heights" may have all seemed the ideal message during a brainstorming session, when applied to an actual event they lack uniqueness and substance as stand-alone slogans. No matter how much money was spent on the theme, attendees return to work and go back to doing exactly what they did before unless you've given them something lasting to think about. It's no wonder most meetings are considered boondoggles and money pits.

How can an event that spans only a few days, or, in some cases, a few hours, be expected to create permanent change? Take physical exercise, for example, I can delude myself into believing that my random four-day spurts of going to the gym should be all I need to have permanent six-pack abs. Sadly, it doesn't. Same for learning. It takes repetition.

The good news? You can create a learning environment that supports good communication and continued learning, where the messaging is repeated, retained, and, most importantly, acted upon. And that is your objective so you meet the objectives of your stakeholders. (And you don't even have to give up carbs!)

Chapter 5 explored five ways to achieve the established event goals, many of which tie directly to creating relevant content. It's the

strategist's job to introduce and manage the Discover
collect metrics multiple times a year, and to build ev
messages to life. If you're inclined to hand off the c
Discovery Process and metrics to the marketing team, bewa.
headed back to the land of logistics. Being an integral part of the
strategy team means being responsible for an integral part of the work.
Besides, you now realize there is more to the process than just sending
out satisfaction surveys and asking logistical questions. Own your new
knowledge, wield it effectively, and use it to everyone's advantage.

For samples of Julian's event design skills in action, visit
www.lwindesign.com.

"Strategic events are the only three-dimensional embodiment of a company's marketing message."

~ CHRISTY LAMAGNA

CHAPTER ELEVEN

Moving on Up!

*"The single biggest problem in communication is
the illusion that it has taken place."*

~GEORGE BERNARD SHAW

Strategic events have the power to turbo-charge sales cycles. When you become one of the key stakeholders who drive events, you're all on equal footing with the others and help to shape this messaging. What you bring to the table is essential to the success of both the sales *and* marketing teams…and the company overall. Without you and your team, sales and marketing would remain two dimensional. With your expertise, the company has the potential to achieve higher goals and greater profits. Welcome to the big leagues!

You can think about sales, marketing, and strategic events as the three legs of a stool. Each is important and has its own part to play, but they work together. When all three are synched up, the seat (your brand) is stable. Conversely, when these supports are not working together, brand integrity can get wonky.

Today, many event planners, marketing teams, and sales organizations operate in silos. When the marketing team gets information on an event, it's likely that it will immediately be passed along to potential attendees by email in the form telling them what *needs* to happen, what people *need* to do. Marketing doesn't tend to invite discussion or input.

When it comes to input from the sales team, typically a few inner-circle team members usually decide how they want things to happen and then someone from the team will eventually, after multiple requests, provide you with a list of attendees they'd like you to invite. Then you won't hear from or see anything from either team again until the night of the event (and most likely at the bar), unless they suddenly surface with urgent last-minute additions, changes, requests, and exceptions that could potentially derail the event you've been working on for months.

Remember Your (Important) Place

Planners execute logistics. Executives make decisions. When Master Strategists are included in the conversation, they become the connective tissue between sales and marketing. They craft, with the event, a unified message and facilitate important company outcomes for sales and the bottom line.

They say the road to hell is paved with good intentions. Well, the road to heaven is paved with a lot of hard work. I'm not implying that achieving a state of strategic bliss will be easy. It requires a firm commitment to your goal of bringing strategy to your organization. And that means taking on some of the heavy lifting and some extra work as you unveil, explain, and implement the strategic process.

Focus on your goal and ignore the obstacles, and there will be quite a few along the way, especially when you begin expanding your influence and reaching into areas that marketing has controlled traditionally. Egos, politics, territorial battles, and invisible, yet powerful, lines between departments are going to surface. I am not suggesting that any of this is going to be easy. What I am stating unequivocally is that it's worth the battle, not only for you, but for the sake of the company.

So how do we get the conversations started?

✧ Let's start with the sales team and what the potential obstacles will be there:

- They are "too busy" to meet with you
- They don't care about events beyond their customer meetings and other limited current involvement
- (You suspect) they don't see you as an equal

❖ What's in it for the sales team to consider your proposed changes?

- Opportunities to make more money
- A chance to beat the competition
- Recognition for being the best

Let's take it a step further and provide a vision of the whole domino effect: A better trained and motivated sales force generates higher sales, triumphs over the competition, captures greater market share, creates happy stockholders, benefits from great PR and press coverage, encounters more customer receptivity, boosts revenue for the company, receives bigger sales incentives, makes a higher income and, finally, gets the chance to do it all over again next year, only better. That should get their attention.

❖ Now we need to weave marketing into the plan. This one's a bit trickier. Their potential obstacles include:

- Territorial issues that thwart collaboration
- Budget wars, as in, "Who's paying for this?"
- They're "too busy" to talk to you

❖ What gets the marketing team's attention?

- Effective campaigns supported by mind share and engagement metrics that the leadership team can boast about
- Increased sales that marketing can connect to their own efforts
- Increased budgets for the next fiscal period

The sales team can prove to be a powerful ally to bring the marketing team to the table (that is, the strategy table where you're now finally seated).

❖ Here are possible talking points to drive that alliance with sales to convince marketing to get on board:

- Marketing campaigns are created to support sales efforts. But how often are the salespeople who rely on the marketing materials given the opportunity to provide input into them, gain an explanation on the messaging in the material and brainstorm on how to best use them?

- An event is an ideal forum to bring marketing messages to life; they should embody the essence of the marketing campaign, utilize the concepts effectively, and by doing so, facilitate the sales process.

- By working together, the marketing team gains valuable feedback and can confidently demonstrate how the campaigns and tools they created were so effective.

Don't these sound-like great reasons for sales and marketing to adopt your strategy and join forces with your team?

The strategic planning team will then be able to effectively steer and execute the event plan, becoming visionaries who bring the messages and environmental design together to inspire the learning, the sharing, and the interaction to help reach the goal. When all three functions, sales, marketing, and strategic events, are working in tandem, leveraging talents, and focusing on goals, the results are exponentially rewarding.

"Think of sales, marketing and strategic events as the three legs of a stool."

~ CHRISTY LAMAGNA

CHAPTER TWELVE

Content and Production

*"Teamwork is the fuel that allows common people
to attain uncommon results."*

~ARISTOTLE

Key Terms for This Chapter:

◈ Production Strategist

◈ Master Show Deck

◈ Voice of God (VOG)

When produced strategically, events become the dynamic intersection of sales and marketing. They are the lynch pin for both departments' successes. By delivering messaging inspired by your target audience's stated pain points, which you collected during Data Discovery, you will engage that audience with content which is meaningful, timely, and motivating.

Well-designed content inspires, informs, engages, and educates. But how do you make sure the environment doesn't interfere with the delivery of content? That is the role of the **production strategist**.

No matter how thorough the planning leading up to the event, once onsite, the pace and intensity ramps up considerably. Traditional planners focus primarily on what happens *outside the ballroom*, F&B, décor, room drops, registration, the avalanche of people and things demanding attention. Traditionally, if it plugs in or lights up, we leave that to the production team to manage. With all those details and attendees demanding attention, the ballroom is easily overlooked. It may even be considered outside the planner's primary responsibilities.

Strategically planned events put equal, if not more, attention on what happens *inside* the ballroom. At least one dedicated production strategist is always stationed inside the ballroom. That means that they arrive when the crew arrives each day, hours before the audience does, and remains there throughout the close of the general session and all the way through rehearsals for the *next* day's activities.

While the ballroom is where the real action is, for planners, the flurry of activity and the noise outside the ballroom tend to beckon and captivate our attention. We think we have to handle everything: Maybe I should direct traffic to the registration desk? Should I solve this signage problem? I should check on the buffet! By contrast, production strategists don't get sucked into any of that stuff. In fact, they often don't even notice it. Their attitude, rightly so, is: "The event strategists assigned to manage onsite logistics will take care of those things." All their energy is dedicated to smooth sailing *inside* the ballroom.

If the steps of the Discovery Process you've completed thus far worked, and your content is engaging your audience, you will see it. Check out the body language: are people smiling, nodding, clapping, taking notes? Or, have they pulled out cell phones or begun to nod off? If all goes as planned, the audience is mindfully tuned in, excited, tracking with the speaker, and the seeds for behavioral change and new habits have been sown. Your post-show communication plan will reinforce what they're learning now so it becomes habit; it will also acknowledge their new behavior and measure the results.

Silos are for Farmers

When someone in an organization is asked, or required, to speak at an event, often they don't get a full rundown of the event's vision, goals, and structure. This is in part because there is often no central repository for this information or, more likely, no one has pulled it together. At an internal sales event, typical general sessions kick off with the CEO. She enters to rousing music, welcomes the audience, and sets an upbeat tone. Then she launches into the state-of-the-organization address, typically designed to highlight and acknowledge past accomplishments, point out trends or challenges, and then psych up the team for what they will be expected to do next for the organization.

One of the most consistent oversights which occurs when designing show content is that each presenter and presentation is developed in a silo, isolated from one another. Speakers focus on their individual content and slides without much awareness of who speaks before or after them and what the other speakers will cover. Some executives believe that information is unnecessary or a distraction to their presenting the latest and greatest from their neck of the woods.

Once a deck is finalized, speakers often upload their slides to a secure site. They may not be able to see other presenters' materials and they may not see their own again until they're presenting them onstage. Someone puts all the presenters' material together in sequential order by day, hands everything over to the production team and turns their attention to onsite logistics. This contextual disconnect contributes to meetings not delivering to their full potential.

Imagine a restaurant where multiple head chefs each create a meal course without the benefit of knowing (or perhaps caring) what the other chefs are preparing. Think of the potential for flavor and texture clashes, missing ingredients, redundant seasoning. To make matters worse, no one has tasted the dishes before they left the kitchen, your server was hired that day, and there was no manager or maître d' to keep things moving smoothly or address problems. Quel désastre! This might be great for the chefs' egos, but not such a great dining experience for the guests. That's the equivalent of what happens when content is designed in silos and presented to the audience without being viewed by someone with an objective eye to view it in the large context. Then it's served up by an in-house production crew without the benefit of a strategist overseeing the entire production. Yep, a disaster! With a dinner gone wrong, you might risk a few hundred dollars; if a general session unravels it can cost a hundred thousand!

Ensuring Quality

Getting all the presenters' slides ahead of time and assembled for the event is a big responsibility and a vital one. It should be managed by someone who understands the specific event goals, the nature of the content, is able to write effectively and edit judiciously under time and political pressure, and can interact with the speakers confidently, yet respectfully.

Even though you likely won't be the one to manage this task, you must understand the importance that it happens, so content and speakers are stage-worthy. Your marketing or communications team may have someone on staff who can take on this task. If you don't have the right talent in-house, ask your production team if they have someone who can assist. If you don't have a resource and are using an in-house production team, email me for recommendations.

Once the **show deck** is assembled, I suggest that it be distributed to all in-house presenters, ideally, at least six weeks before the meeting with clear instructions that, once finalized, this will be the only deck that will be accepted and presented. This deck coordinates the slides for each speaker in the right order of presentation with the right fonts and font sizes for headlines, subheads, and body copy. It can accommodate images and set the formatting for captions, tables, and other call-outs and annotations. Someone should also make sure the animations are working correctly. There is a template of a master show deck in the Strategic Resource Library.

Unfortunately, most speakers won't look at the template until just before the due date. So be prepared to have material come in past deadline, incorrectly formatted, with a note indicating that they are still waiting for confirmation on a couple of things. You can send it back for completion, insist it be restructured to meet the template guidelines, or let it go if you trust the integrity of the speaker. Plan to resend the deck multiple times because people will claim to have not received it, but don't let that deter you from sending it out early. This accomplishes two things: it sets the stage for a much earlier due date than most are used to, and it clearly establishes what is expected and when.

Professional speakers may not be willing to use a deck branded with your corporate logo. You will likely need to give professional speakers a bit more leeway in terms of their presentation branding, content, and format than you might with internal company speakers—particularly if the speaker's brand is part of their cache.

When the decks are finalized, someone needs to again, review all the decks and, based on the intended messaging of the presentation, suggest or set the order of the speakers. Key executives may have established places on the agenda. Creating a logical content flow around them ensures content is more easily absorbed. Not sure how to do this? Think of each presentation as a chapter in a book. What information needs to be shared first so that the material which follows makes sense? If you notice redundant or conflicting content, contact the speakers and address it.

This is why it is useful to set the deadline for sending in presentations earlier than has previously been allowed, so you have time to coordinate the materials and check for problems or overlaps and work with presenters if something needs to be addressed. There will still be jump drives with presentation decks being loaded into the show computer as the speaker takes the stage, but that will become the exception not the rule.

You are likely to get push back about earlier deadlines from your presenters. If no one has ever reviewed their decks before, expect some people to be appreciative and others annoyed. With your key stakeholders' new appreciation for well-curated content, as a means to influence behavior and achieve goals, you have the support you need as people adapt to the new system and deadlines.

In-house or Out-house?

With this perspective on the critical nature of content development and curation, let's address the question of using an in-house production team (that the hotel has on property) versus hiring a third-party vendor (this assumes you will have vetted them ahead of time or you have worked successfully with them before). See where I'm going here: Do you really want to wait until the day before your show to meet the (in-house) venue team that will be responsible for making your presenters look and sound good? My third-party production partners have been with me at many events, from the initial site inspection and theming to the post-show wrap-up call. They know my event goals and are instrumental in creating a ballroom atmosphere that ensures my company will achieve them. I trust them with my reputation.

I admit that there are many talented in-house production crews at various venues around the world. The challenge is you won't know who you're getting until you're onsite, as most in-house production managers can't commit to who will be assigned to your show until a few weeks out.

As someone who likes to make sure things go smoothly, that makes me very nervous. Rehearsals are not the time for the crew to meet your executives for the first time and try then to get a sense of their style. It takes a little time to learn who tends to rush through slides or who gets sidetracked and runs late, or who always wants to walk out to an Elton John song but can never figure out which one until moments before she takes the stage. You want to relax knowing that the speakers' names will be pronounced correctly by the person doing the **"Voice of God"** **(VOG)** announcements. But it's up to you. If you're okay with a 'roll of the dice' philosophy when it comes to executing your events' most critical services, that's fine. But then perhaps we should start over at Chapter 1.

Not convinced? Here's another oldie but goodie from my chest of war stories:

We were putting on an event at a well-known and highly regarded hotel in New York City. The client was paying an exorbitant rate because of the name and the history of the building, but it made the desired impression on their guests. We found out early in the process that we could bring in our production team, but it had to be at a 1:1 ratio. So, for every person we brought in from the outside, we needed to also hire a union person that the venue chose as well. Even though we didn't need the extra hands, ours were tied. It was expensive for sure, but worse than that, relying on people we'd never met to produce the show was a gamble.

During load in, I met the in-house audio person. He was an energetic young man who enthusiastically shook my hand. He told me he was thrilled to be part of our crew, especially since he had just been promoted to production the previous week. He'd been a bellman for the last six months. He was 'super excited' to learn more about AV. I was not super excited. Furthermore, he was being billed out at a rate that would have turned your hair white.

The show loaded in and we had a 5 a.m. crew call. Our team was assigned to the key run of show positions: stage managing, technical director, audio lead, etc. The in-house team was there with us, but- we had photographic evidence that, of the four people mandatorily hired to work with us, three of them were sleeping during that initial meeting. Later, when we presented the pictures to the manager of the onsite team, he was neither surprised nor embarrassed and said it had no bearing on the invoice.

This experience was extreme but not entirely unexpected. Onsite show crews cannot be vetted. In-house production teams have a high turnover rate and are most likely using equipment that has been overused. Venues charge the standard tax and service fees on top of the production crew's rates, which always includes a percentage for the venue. (It could be upwards of 28% depending on where the event is held.)

In-house providers are focused on volume, not precision. How could it be otherwise, with no time to work with clients in advance and new ones arriving each week? It's not the production team's fault; they are just doing their jobs. The system is setup for profit, not artistry. Some hotels, like several I know of in Las Vegas, took in-house production requirement a step beyond; they prohibited us from using our own people and equipment and made using theirs mandatory. Avoid that situation if you can. Why gamble on the caliber of crew and equipment and pay extra for the privilege?

To be fair, there are talented professionals who work for in-house production organizations. But my point is that there are no guarantees. The odds of getting in-house lighting or audio designers who are masters of their craft is lower than if you hire an outside company whose work you know. If you work with a vendor show after show, they rely on your repeat business and their good reputation to survive. So, they will protect yours.

If you're new to the idea of working with a production team and not sure where to start, visit the Strategic Resource Library for a hiring cheat sheet. You'll also find my time-trusted guideline document on how to manage a general session with confidence.

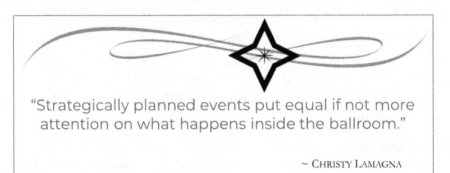

"Strategically planned events put equal if not more attention on what happens inside the ballroom."

~ CHRISTY LAMAGNA

CHAPTER THIRTEEN

Planning Your Future

"The question isn't who is going to let me;
the question is who is going to stop me."

~AYN RAND

Key Terms for This Chapter:

✦ Strategic Planning Movement

Achieving goals is the result of patience, perseverance, and hard work. Yes, there may be some luck in there, but as Henry Ford put it, "The harder I work, the luckier I get." Becoming a strategist and inspiring your organization to follow a strategic event path is a lofty aspiration and will take some hard work. But, that is what makes the process so exciting and the achievement so sweet when you get there.

Imagine Your Future, Then Step Into It

The benefits and power of strategic thinking are certainly not limited to events. They can apply to everything in life. The key is having a goal and gearing all your actions toward crossing the finish line. (Then, of course, you can set your sights on the *next* awesome thing you want to accomplish.) Inviting strategic thinking into how you view and solve challenges is the first step toward not just a more fulfilling professional life, but also a richer and more meaningful whole life.

Ask yourself: How do I feel on Sunday nights and Monday mornings? Are you eager to start a new work week or desperately trying to avoid thinking about it? What goes through your mind when you think of your career?

If you're not sure, here's an exercise that might help:

Make a list of all the things you love about your job, the company or clients you work with, your team, and your role as an event professional. Now, make a list of the challenges, frustrations and things you'd like to change. (You can do this while commuting, running on a treadmill, waiting for yet another delayed flight to depart, or instead of listening to a whining friend complain about her love life, *again*.)

Let's look at your list. Does it contain phrases which indicate frustration, disappointment, or alienation? I've been tracking a trend in our industry lately. Lots of articles and other media seem to focus on topics like: "doing more with less," "getting a seat at the table," "avoiding burnout," "handling difficult co-workers," "earning respect," "asking for a raise," and so on. Lots. The event industry seems to be full of frustrated people. I would like to speculate that this is a symptom of the limited scope planners have enjoyed and the value they have been given historically. It follows that logistics-focused events which cost companies money without producing any meaningful ROI create a domino effect of disappointment, from the planner to the attendee to the C-suite to vendor partners and back to planners, a truly vicious cycle.

At this point, you know strategic planning transforms event spending, an investment that supports sales cycles, influences behavior, and achieves important, stated goals. When you plan *strategically*, you are effectively eliminating some key *causes* of the frustration, not treating the *symptoms*. This applies to hoteliers, vendor partners, third-party planners, corporate planners, DMCs, CVBs, speaker's bureaus, florists, CMOs, sales managers, you name it—pretty much the entire hospitality industry. We will *all* benefit by adopting this process.

Will adopting a strategic approach whiten your teeth, de-frizz your hair, or shorten your commute? I don't know about the first two, but it could allow you to work from home on occasion. More directly though, if you feel that you have more work than there are hours, more tasks than hands to complete them, a sense of being under appreciated and underpaid, being in an almost constant state of overwhelm and exhaustion, then transforming yourself into an event or Master

Strategist *can* help. It will shorten your career-negatives list. Better still, your list of positives will grow longer. What do you have to lose?

Imagine how it would feel to have the respect, influence, and significance you crave. How would your day-to-day work life be different? What would your office look like? It could change what you wear, how you walk, and how often you smile. Once you can truly imagine yourself having what you want, you'll already start changing your environment. Surround yourself with powerful, positive reminders that the "new you" is already stepping up and stepping in with each effort you put forth.

One thing that is important to mention is you don't have to make this transition overnight or do it alone. Like most journeys, they are more fun when you enjoy the process and have people along with you to share it. Get your team involved and on board. Share these ideas with colleagues across the industry. Share your triumphs, but also your challenges—because if you're feeling frustrated, chances are others have experienced it too and can offer suggestions for new approaches. Hey, create a groundswell. Energy creates more energy, so create the spark that ignites change not just for yourself, but also for your colleagues, your partners, your organization, and for the entire industry.

Check out this community of people already taking on this same challenge and thriving, **Strategic Planning Movement**: https://www.linkedin.com/groups/8652469/. Add your voice, share your story and help inspire others with your successes, perseverance, and big ideas.

Perception is Reality

I truly believe that this is our industry's time to make some big changes and take the reins of our fate into our own hands.

In the 1950s, "stewardess" was the accepted term for the *women* who staffed airline cabins and tended to passenger needs. The general perception was that stewardesses were "flying waitresses" or, worse, "eye candy," which overshadowed their primary responsibility: passenger safety. In the 1960s and 1970s, there was a unified push to replace the term with the gender-free "flight attendant" moniker. The move was fueled by the growing discontent among women with sexism and the influx of more men into the industry.

The push for change went beyond a new title. Trained and talented industry professionals came together with a shared goal of changing perceptions and how they were treated by customers and their companies. They demanded to be portrayed with a more accurate picture of the importance and scope of their role. Perception is reality. For the reality of their jobs and their level of respect to change, they needed people's perceptions to change.

Today women pilots are not an uncommon sight (although it would be great to see more of them). What an evolution!

This drive for validation and recognition turned into a campaign for licensing. The respect a profession earns when its practitioners must be licensed to legally perform the prescribed tasks or services is substantial. It took the terrorist attacks of September 11th—when the need for safety rose to unprecedented levels—to make flight attendant licensure a reality, but it finally happened.

My vision of success for our industry might seem a bit radical, but it calls for formal licensing for strategic event professionals. Perhaps it will be driven by a similar factor: safety.

Playing it Safe

Safety is also a key factor in our industry. Since 2001, it's not only the skies that became backdrops for organized violence. Schools, churches, concerts, gaming conventions, festivals, events of all sizes, both public and private, have become potential targets for terrorism and violence.

Establishing a comprehensive safety plan, with detailed procedures and protocols for events, is a required task for events in today's world. A painful correlation is emerging around events and the need for safety plans. The unthinkable is becoming more and more common. If you bring groups of people together without having developed a solid safety plan, it's not only irresponsible, it's also negligent and potentially criminal.

We are responsible for the safety of those who entrust us with their lives each time they step into one of our events. Whether it's entering an unfamiliar hotel property or an off-site facility, sitting below lighting and other gear hung above on trusses, eating food we select and prepare, stepping onto shuttles or boats we arrange, and so on. Therefore, it is incumbent upon us to make sure that the events we produce are not only meaningful and impactful, but safe.

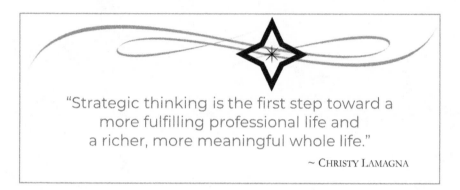

"Strategic thinking is the first step toward a more fulfilling professional life and a richer, more meaningful whole life."

~ CHRISTY LAMAGNA

CHAPTER FOURTEEN

Coming Together as an Industry

"You can't make a cake without breaking a few eggs."

~UNKNOWN

Formal licensing for strategic event professionals from all sectors of the industry may be a distant goal, but there are plenty of changes which can and should occur along that path. Change, however, no matter how beneficial the result, often includes some discomfort. If we are genuinely committed to raising the standards for our industry and its practitioners to new heights, we must make some unpopular decisions.

Even without formal licensure in place, stricter standards could protect event attendees from the work of those who are not sufficiently qualified. There should be a standards organization with the power to sanction those who do not perform up to a certain established baseline of acceptable behavior and integrity. That could even include: executive admins who do planning on the side, the fly-by-night companies who cut corners to win bids only to disappoint, or worse, endanger staff or attendees and give the industry a bad reputation. It could prevent those nice, well-meaning "solopreneurs" who anoint themselves as planners from attempting corporate level projects just because they threw a few anniversary and wedding shindigs. Don't get me wrong: party planners have valuable skills and should be proud of the parties they plan and execute. But that should not be confused with what strategic event professionals do. That's why they have different titles.

If you're an executive admin who is furious at me right now for suggesting you aren't qualified to occasionally plan events for your boss just because you don't do this full time, let me put it this way: Suppose I came to your office and claimed that I know as much as you do about administering an executive's office because I can type and answer the phone. I'd be so wrong, because there is so much more, so many nuances, to what you do. In fact, you likely do things so seamlessly, that it looks easy or transparent. That's the same for my profession. If you're as good and committed as you feel you are to event planning—heck, you're reading this book--then perhaps you *should* be doing this full time. So, join us and do what you love year-round, not just sporadically. We'd love to have you join us.

Julius Erving (the famous basketball player known as "Dr. J") once said, "I firmly believe that respect is a lot more important, and a lot greater, than popularity." I couldn't agree more, and those who are committed to evolving and igniting their careers, no matter what field they're in, know that to be true as well. If you believe in the goal, you must be willing to do the work. Other people's hurt feelings and power struggles are distractions. Remedy that by sharing your vision and inviting others to come along. Those who prefer to put their energy into emotional battles because it's the easier option are self-selecting out.

Setting Higher Standards

Let's summarize on safety, competence, and licensing and what it could mean to our industry overall.

Hundreds of people put their lives in our hands at each event. They trust the hotel has been vetted for bedbugs, the food has been correctly labeled in case they have allergies, the location is safe, the people working onsite are responsible and that we will meet their needs throughout their stay.

The people we hire and partner with must reflect our sense of professionalism. We are only as good as our weakest link. They must be well trained, calm under pressure, and able to responsibly manage budgets and negotiate contracts. They must have the flexibility and resourcefulness to interact with executives, vendors, attendees, and random strangers who wander into event spaces. They must see the big picture and effectively compartmentalize challenges, so their focus isn't derailed, and they can attend to details.

I find that I work best with colleagues, partners and even vendors whose commitment and energy levels are similar to mine (people who know me will confirm that's pretty high). There is also a long list of skills I look for in those who will need to be able to execute the thousands of logistical tasks for every event. When I bring someone onto my event team, I am bestowing on them tremendous trust and great responsibility for managing tasks and people with the utmost care, respect, and expertise. I feel strongly that this job, done right, isn't something that can be accomplished between other tasks or divvied up between various people whose primary focus and skills lie elsewhere.

We must cultivate a shared industry vocabulary to effectively articulate who we are and what we do, particularly if we are going to truly change perceptions of *our* work. That is necessary if we are to engender sufficient confidence and trust in our organizations such that we can shift the behaviors of our executives and our event attendees.

Many organizations don't set expectations for strategic planning or strategic attendance at events. How can we help to move these organizations forward?

We can certainly draw on best practices from event strategists across the industry and the world; there are more of them stepping up every year to establish this new standard for accomplishment and recognition. But there are still many areas that require attention and correction.

We all expend so much energy on executing perfect plans, yet it seems there is no plan to come together as an industry to support each other and lift each other up. The silos we struggle with in our organizations are seen all over our industry and need to come down.

It's up to us. Ask yourself: To what extent do I consider the industry and my status in it a challenge? What am I willing to do to change it? How much empathy do I have for my colleagues who are struggling and how much energy am I willing to expend to make a difference?

There are event strategists around the world who have committed to helping create change and whose lives have changed since they started thinking and planning strategically. I've found many of them and know they're willing to share their ideas and best practices. Many of them have contributed to this book. I started the Strategic Planning Movement to bring individuals who want to make changes together, and I speak throughout the country on how to begin the process. I've touched thousands of people and have barely scratched the surface. Interested in joining the effort or being featured for the strategic work you're doing? If so, get in touch!

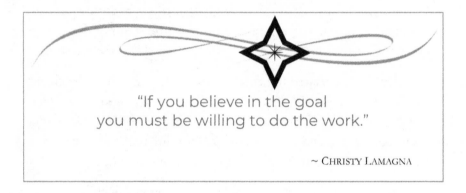

"If you believe in the goal
you must be willing to do the work."

~ CHRISTY LAMAGNA

CHAPTER FIFTEEN

Collecting and Connecting

"I've learned that people will forget what you said, people will forget what you did, but people will never forget how you made them feel."

~MAYA ANGELOU

Key Terms for This Chapter:

✧ Collecting and Connecting®

It's What You Know AND Who You Know

Intelligence is not about having all the answers. It is about knowing how to find them. We are constantly fielding questions whose answers are often beyond our scope of direct knowledge. Fortunately, most of us find pleasure in the pursuit of the impossible, have fantastic network connections and can usually find someone who knows the answer or can suggest a response. We also have some great stories associated with the random requests we've received and successfully handled over our careers.

Although tactical by nature, logistics are an integral component of any strategic plan. As part of that plan, they are executed with the goal in mind. The requests we get don't follow a plan. In fact, they can border on the truly bizarre. Knowing how to diffuse what can turn into a wild goose chase without getting anyone's feathers ruffled is another element of being strategic. Wasting time is wasting money, and that is the opposite of being strategic. So how do you deflect requests that you know are going to distract you from accomplishing your goals? I'll show you how and then give you some opportunities to practice.

❖ Let us first pay tribute to some of the random requests my colleagues and I have received over the years:

- "Can we ship 1,000 mannequins to your office?"
- "Do we need a permit to walk a camel down a New York City street?"
- "Where can we rent a steamroller, and do we need a special license to drive it?"
- "Who makes the world's best soccer balls, and can we get 300 next month?"
- "Can we get a cadaver shipped to the ballroom?"
- "Can you have a helicopter here in an hour?"
- "What would the hotel charge us to change the wallpaper in the ballroom?"
- "If we remove the plate glass window at the front of the hotel, do you think we could display a car in the lobby?"
- "I know we're on a private jet to L.A., but is there any way we can stop for chocolate ice cream?"
- "Would an alligator survive if we put one in the hotel's pool or would the chlorine hurt it?"
- "How many gallons of Jell-O™ will it take to fill the outdoor hot tub?"
- "Is there any chance we can get Morgan Freeman to record the voiceover for our corporate video...tomorrow?"

I swear these are true. Amazingly, we handled them all to the client's satisfaction. Now that does NOT mean doing what was originally asked, but we came as close as was reasonably (or legally) possible. When it's up to you to make the magic happen, you're going to need to do whatever it takes, and that usually involves bringing in additional resources.

Send me your favorite random client request. I know there are countless gems just waiting to be shared and I'd love to hear them.

People are the Most Abundant Resource on Earth

Achieving success when attempting the impossible often comes down to who you know. Keeping up my network of trusted resources has proven priceless throughout my career. I usually know right away who to call when I get an off-the-wall request. Not only that, but I'm proud to say I have accumulated enough random knowledge over time to have become the "go-to" person for others on their own wild goose chases. You don't have to be the person who knows everything or even knows everyone, just be someone who people want in their network. Quid pro quo.

If your network isn't as robust as you'd like, or you aren't seen as a "go-to" by others, I think I can help. Perhaps you struggle with making and keeping connections. Perhaps you've even attended organized networking events and felt awkward and intimidated. If so, you're not alone. People go to networking events with the simple goal of meeting new people for an assortment of purposes. They arrive eager and ready to schmooze, but upon crossing the threshold, a metamorphosis occurs. Those who might normally be outgoing are suddenly seized with shyness and can't imagine starting a conversation. Others behave as if they were on a game show where the person who doles out or collects the most business cards wins. Some people head straight for the buffet or bar...and stay there. They're playing their own individual competitive sport: how much can I eat and/or drink in two hours, so I don't have to talk to anyone. Bonus points for making no eye contact. There are a few people who attend who are comfortable meeting new people, even enjoy it. And they often put others at ease in making conversation as well. We love them and hate them...but mostly, we'd like to be them.

It may come as a surprise to my colleagues and friends, but I fall into that first category. Put me in front of an audience and I can joyfully speak for hours. Ask me to walk into a room and network with strangers and every cell in my body screams, "RETREAT!" Since I run a company, I don't have the option of eliminating networking events from my schedule. I must go. And once there, I can't behave like a wallflower or wear a pained expression on my face all evening. I can't eat all the prosciutto and drink six glasses of red wine. I have to be able to carry on a quality conversation.

I'll share a secret that helped me. I realized that I get energy from helping people, but I wouldn't ask a stranger for a glass of water if my hair were on fire. I used to go to these events because I felt obligated as my company's CEO to meet new potential clients or partners. At that time, my WIIFM was checking off the box that I'd gone, and then escaping before I was cornered by the sales guy collecting everyone's business cards.

So, I decided to look at things differently, to start with my desired outcome and work backward. This is usually a good first step in figuring out how to reach a goal, so I thought about *my* goal. My WIIFM in life is to teach, inspire, and assist. I enjoy meeting people when I feel I can help them in some way. Once I realized that, I stopped "networking" for the sake of it and started doing what I call **Collecting and Connecting**.

Collecting and Connecting is a giving-based philosophy that centers on finding ways to bring people together and help them achieve their goals. So in becoming a resource for others, I win. I feed my natural desire to connect people who may have never met otherwise, find ways to help them reach *their* goals, and comfortably expand my circle at the same time. And it creates good karma.

I now walk confidently into rooms and introduce myself to strangers because I realize every conversation is an opportunity, not for business per se, but to help. I listen more than I speak, ask follow-up questions and go through my mental database of people and resources that may help the person in front of me.

I've turned it into a game that has multiple winners and countless rewards. Connecting people has led them to new jobs, writing and speaking opportunities, and even love. I've connected pet parents and dog walkers, bespoke tailors to the clothing challenged, a personal chef to a group of gourmet vegans…the list is endless. Each time I make an introduction, I authentically add someone to my network. Being a resource for others is of equal, if not more, value than *my* having resources to call upon. Here's a nice example:

Steve, a local contractor, worked on a show that my company was producing. With his exceptional video production skills, he was an excellent addition to our onsite team. That caught my attention and led to our having a few 1:1 conversations. I added Steve to my network and made a mental note to keep in touch with him. Some years went by without our having the opportunity to work together. One afternoon, Steve called me. "Hey Christy, I know we haven't talked in a while, but I need some help with something and I thought if anyone could help me on this, it's Christy!"

Steve did need help, and fast. He explained that he needed to find someone who spoke Chinese, and English, and could jump on a flight (by private jet) within a week and head to China to act as a translator for an important event he was working on. My only question was, "Are any specific dialects required?" Within two days I was able to give Steve the names of two people who could potentially help. He hired one and off they went.

Steve earned rock star status with his client, I helped someone get a lucrative gig and was able to do Steve a favor, and all while doing something I love: Collecting and Connecting. The bonus is that if Steve thinks of me for random requests like that—when he needs a company to plan an event or hears that someone needs a speaker or coach, Strategic Meetings & Events and I are at the top of his list.

If you embrace the collecting-and-connecting approach, I'm confident it will prove endlessly helpful throughout your life. In fact, if you want to add me to your network, email me. I'm happy to be a resource and connect with you.

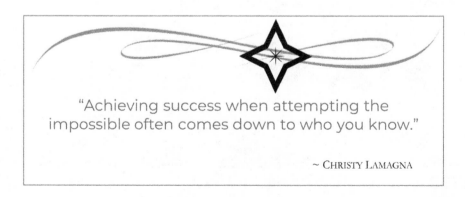

"Achieving success when attempting the impossible often comes down to who you know."

~ Christy Lamagna

CHAPTER SIXTEEN

Strategic Sponsorships

"Optimism is the faith that leads to achievement"

~HELEN KELLER

Sponsor dollars are the financial backbone for many shows. However, gone are the days when sponsors would fund lavish affairs (think closing night bands that cost six figures at a party complete with caviar, vodka, and luges). Many organizations now rely on sponsor money just for general operating expenses, never mind extras. Falling short could even mean canceling the event. Or if you're working with an external audience, it could mean raising the registration price to a level where you lose attendees who can't afford to come.

There's good news and bad news if you're still offering three tiers of sponsorship—say, Platinum, Gold, and Silver packages—where each includes some combination of traditional promotional opportunities (like a sponsor logo on social media pages, sponsor name on a lanyard, mention from the podium, etc.). The bad news is you're stuck in the 80s and you're likely missing out on better opportunities. The good news is that Discovery Sessions and Data Discovery can help bring your sponsorship chops up to par.

Designing custom packages for sponsors will inject new life and dollars into your events. You can meet with your key stakeholders and establish your sponsorship goals, which may include:

- Hard-dollar revenue, perhaps as an increase from previous years (by amount or percentage)

- In-kind donations (equipment, giveaways, services, etc.)

- Leads / contacts for ideal organizations or business sectors to target

- An increase in the number or prestige of sponsoring organizations

Whether an organization is a current or potential sponsor, you should be clear on *their* goals and how you can help achieve them. Even if you think you already know, make the effort to confirm. I suggest opening the conversation with, "How can we tailor a sponsorship package to best help you achieve *your* sales and marketing goals at this event?"

With this approach, you will leapfrog the yes or no part, and, instead, find yourself and the sponsor enthusiastically brainstorming and exploring details of the sponsorship. It's quite a contrast to the dusty, old recitation of a list of fixed offerings that inevitably receives a lifeless "I'll get back to you" in response—and often doesn't. Even better, instead of having to nag sponsors for an agreement, how exciting would it be if they called you the next time?

Some companies want to place a product sample into potential customers' hands. Others may covet face-to-face interaction with your attendees. Or, perhaps they wish to position their organization as a thought leader in their industry. There are many, many interesting options to mix and match: a high-level cocktail party, a spot in a golf foursome, a seat at an off-site or awards dinner, the opportunity to host a VIP reception.

If the company has a story they want to tell, you can offer a preshow podcast, a seminar slot, a full-page interview in the show guide, an on-air appearance on the event's YouTube channel or website—that is, as long as the content they supply is not an overt advertisement, which falls into a different category. And on and on. Whatever innovative exposure you can offer them, (within your guidelines, of course) that allows them to demonstrate their unique value to your attendees could be the inspiration they need to sign on the dotted line. Of course, you want to be careful not to create the impression that your event endorses one sponsor's company or products over another's, so be mindful of people's perception.

Curious Minds Find Creative Opportunities

If you are responsible for landing new sponsors and don't know where to start, consider organizations that are natural partners with your product or service. For instance, a sports apparel manufacturer may align itself with a producer of sports drinks, wearable fitness trackers, supplement or power bar manufacturers, sports balm companies, wireless headphone manufacturers, national vitamin store chains, national gyms and so forth.

Finding organizations that go after the same target market as yours, but for different segments of their budget, are natural allies. These relationships can become reciprocal, giving each party the opportunity to gain exposure with the other's audience. Why not explore cross-sponsoring each other's events or going in on an event together and co-sponsoring something at a large tradeshow? You can leverage each other's spend and audience. This taps into several of the principles we've discussed: WIIFM, Collecting and Connecting, asking how you can help someone solve a problem, asking what people want and then giving it to them to form lasting alliances.

Another strategy is to go in an entirely different direction and find products or services that are unrelated to yours but resonate with your audience. Consider a car manufacturer, fitness chain, wealth advisor. If your target audience is interested in a product or service, companies that offer them are sponsorship candidates. You are also providing an unexpected element of WIIFM for your audience. Add a question on your next post-show survey that asks for suggestions of sponsors your attendees would find useful. Why guess when the answers are only a question away?

"Designing custom packages for sponsors will inject new life and dollars into you events."

~ CHRISTY LAMAGNA

CHAPTER SEVENTEEN

Strategic Thinking for Hotels, Vendors, and Third-party Providers

"There is immense power when a group of people with similar interests gets together to work toward the same goals."

~IDOWU KOYENIKAN

Key Terms for This Chapter:

- ✦ Strategic Objectives
- ✦ Request for Proposal (RFP)
- ✦ Banquet Event Orders (BEO)
- ✦ Destination Management Company (DMC)
- ✦ Convention and Visitors Bureaus (CVB)
- ✦ Destination Marketing Organization (DMO)

The need for strategic thinking and its benefits are applicable to the entire hospitality industry. Hotels, off-site venues, and all the vendors who bring their specific talents and expertise to help create the event. The better their understanding of the event's goals and for whom the event is being produced, the more effective they can be. Remember, all decisions and program elements need to be made with the goal in mind. That rule applies to everyone associated with the event. To avoid miscommunication with our own team and partner ecosystem, SME created our "**Strategic Objectives**" document that identifies an event's goals and target audience. We share it with all our vendors. There's a copy in the Strategic Resource Library for you to download and start using.

Be More than Their Guest

Savvy hotel sales directors and convention service managers will jump at an opportunity to be more integral in creating your event experience beyond just completing a **request for proposal (RFP)** and creating **banquet event orders**, **(BEOs)**. Take advantage of this. Share your vision with the hotel and ask them how to best utilize their space, staff, and talents to help create the optimal onsite experience. When you ask for the details on a room you're considering for a reception, that's the information you'll be given. But if you explain the goal of the meeting, you allow your hotel partner to imagine how best to place the activities and to service them. Let the experts do their jobs and allow them to get creative. This gives them the opportunity to host your meeting rather than just hold it.

> *James was working with a large group at an upscale hotel in Florida. The outdoor space by the pool wasn't suitable for the welcome reception, but he and the client agreed that holding the event indoors was not really an option either as that would rob their attendees of the breathtaking beauty of a Florida fall sunset. James shared the challenge with his CSM, who had suggested they meet and walk the space together. They were passing through the porte-cochere (the place where cars drive through) when they both realized that it would be the perfect place for the reception. The hotel had never considered using that space for that purpose. Afterwards, when the hotel saw how wildly successful James' welcome reception was, they started marketing the space as part of their rentable inventory!*

Venues can be places that just *contain* meetings, or they can be spaces that *transform* them into a memorable experience. Work with your hotel team to imagine spaces beyond what you see and look to them for their potential ability to enhance your program and support your goals.

Pro Tip:

Bring someone from your production team to site visits. They'll not only help imagine and design the event's look and feel, they'll also ask questions you might not think of, such as those pertaining to the back of the house, which will affect your ballroom set design, set up, and load out. You can get a jump on this, by familiarizing yourself with the list of things production teams typically look for onsite. Find it in the Strategic Resource Library.

Food is a Key Ingredient to Successful Event Design

The chef is another resource that many people under-utilize. Chefs are imaginative, creative people who usually appreciate being engaged on event challenges. Sharing with them the program's theme and goals, and providing details around evening events, receptions, or award dinners, may inspire off-menu dishes, clever centerpieces, custom desserts and more. These ideas might seem purely logistical, but they can truly be strategic if they help advance the event's established goals.

Production Vendors

We've established that production teams hold your show content in their hands. If you have a dedicated production vendor, share your goals and ask them to suggest stage sets, lighting packages, show themes, clever entrances, or product reveals. Let them work their magic. The earlier you bring them into the process, the more helpful they can be.

Destination Management Companies

Destination management companies (DMCs) can be amazingly helpful when it comes to creating elements that support your goals and your event design. Include them in more than just designing around the theme for the final night party. If the DMC is well connected, they may be able to suggest and source creative ideas you've never imagined were possible, and it's likely that the resources will be local.

Convention and Visitors' Bureaus

We've established that **convention and visitors' bureaus (CVBs)** (also known as **destination management companies**, or **DMCs**), are experts on facilities and services in your host city. Explain your goals and challenges to them to find creative ways to leverage the city's facilities and services and those in the surrounding areas to support your goals.

Ben is the CEO of a high-end cookware company. His online sales were strong, but in-store sales through distributors were lagging. The goal we agreed on was to bring those numbers up by 12% over the next calendar year.

During Data Discovery, it was revealed that distributors found communication lacking on new products. Not only were shipments arriving past the confirmed roll-out dates, the in-store marketing materials announcing the new products were rather underwhelming, making it harder to build any excitement around the launches. The organization's pledge was to improve communication and to meet deadlines. In return, the distributors were being asked to prominently showcase the company's new products, so they would receive more attention. When we explained this to the DMC, they suggested we take a tour of QVC Studios in West Chester, PA. We arranged to do just that. The QVC tour showcased one of the largest and best run sales and marketing empires in the world. It communicates with its viewers/customers in real time, 24-7. It's as close to a seamless process as a company could hope to achieve. The contact at the DMC made this helpful and informative suggestion without even understanding our goals.

Ben and the team left excited, inspired, and ready to revisit how their operation was run. After seeing what a giant like QVC could accomplish, their challenges seemed more than fixable. They left with a desire to achieve even loftier goals and excited about what was possible.

Florals, Décor and Priorities, Oh My!

Once you become goal-driven, you are likely to discover that some activities that have taken up a good deal of your time are no longer part of your focus. Florals, for instance, may be a target for re-prioritizing or outsourcing. Décor, too, may take a backseat to other pressing strategic elements. Of course, that depends on the industry your company is in.

For some industries, aesthetics is an integral part of the environment. If you're in the beauty industry, for example, florals do matter. Once you know where you're headed, you can re-prioritize tasks, and let the less important ones fade into the background.

Strategic thinking leads to more efficient spending. This new focus sometimes results in budget shifts and can even create a surplus. That's not to say that your previous spending was entirely wasted (you have to figure into the value equation the experience you're leveraging now). It just means you may have been putting too much emphasis on details which didn't warrant that much attention. Perhaps the final night dinner needs top-quality décor, but perhaps it warrants two instead of five hours for the table scape design. You can put that extra three hours towards other details that are more goal related.

Giveaways

People like stuff. Some even expect it. Often it doesn't matter what it is, we just like getting it. I've worked countless tradeshows where someone will ask for two of the giveaway items before they even know what it is. Tradeshows offer an adult version of trick-or-treating. But countless dollars can be wasted on promotional items that don't extend a brand's message or bring the company's products to life.

If you are going to supply giveaways, you may want to partner with a sponsor who wants your audience to experience a sample of their product or offers something bearing their logo which attendees will enjoy using (thus linking the warm and fuzzy feeling with their brand). If your goal is to create a lasting impression, it's important to know that T-shirts and ball caps often get handed off to attendees' kids, mugs break on the way home, and pens end up in a desk drawer. Bottom line; they don't achieve the goal.

If you're going to put your own or a sponsor's dollars into a giveaway, put some thought into what conveys the right message and represents the brand. Hopefully it's something they'll want to hold on to and use visibly.

Ask yourself: What was the best giveaway item I ever received? Why did I like it? Do I still have it and use it? If so, does it make me think about the company that gave it to me? Would the same type of item resonate with my audience?

I once received an emergency kit for my car as a giveaway from an auto insurance company. It was chock full of cool, useful gadgets most drivers would like to have on hand but don't often spend money on: flares, a magnetic flashlight that could be used as a safety flare, and reflective triangles. The message was, "[Name of the Company] is there with you when you need us." Perfect. What can you offer your attendees that will create an appropriate and long-lasting positive impression?

Pro tip:

Explore creating a company-wide online portal to source all giveaway items. Having a single source for promotional items insures brand integrity, offers controls and tracks spending, and can be used to leverage total annual spend. Work with your preferred vendor to offer rebates based on spending tiers and suggest to management that those dollars be used towards event team salary increases, bonuses, or new hires.

"Venues can be places that just contain meetings,
or they can be spaces that transform them
into a memorable experience."

~ CHRISTY LAMAGNA

CHAPTER EIGHTEEN

The Art of Having Difficult Conversations

"The art of communication is the language of leadership."

~JAMES HUMES

Have you been in situations where people pretended to like a bad idea because an important person thought of it and no one had the guts to speak up? Depending on the corporate culture, it can be dangerous to disagree with an executive; you risk putting a target on your forehead. Ironically, it might be easier to disrupt an entire industry than it is to disrupt a single department's status quo. When you're upending an industry you don't have to worry about being politically correct.

What do you do when a client or executive wants to hold an event in Hawaii because his or her spouse has been dying to go there? What if the client insists that the entire event be carb-free because their CEO just went on the Paleo diet? Ideally, returning to the goal should put the conversation back into alignment, but we're dealing with the real world here, and not everything goes according to plan. For that reason, you may want to have a few back-pocket ideas ready just in case.

Random vs. Reasonable, Noble vs. Feasible

Remember that list of random (but true) requests clients have made of my team that I shared in Chapter 15? Number one was: "Can we ship 1,000 mannequins to your office?" It sounded crazy, but the back story was actually quite noble. They wanted to stage the mannequins to represent the number of people killed by automatic weapons during a specific time period. I understood their 'WHY" and I agreed that the imagery would have been powerful, but I needed to help them understand that the "HOW' was not feasible.

One cannot always do that directly without creating friction. Instead of entirely dismissing the idea, I jumped on board and began asking questions to see if we could uncover an approach worth serious reconsideration. I told them that my office was too small, but I could investigate renting a space and send them the costs. Did they want to take the mannequins out of the crates to save space or have them stored in the containers until the event? Should I rent a forklift to get the crates into the box truck to move them or did they have one? (I knew they did not.) Should we hire staff to dress the mannequins, or would they be able to get 50 volunteers for eight hours each to do that? What about the clothing: sponsored or purchased? And after the event: ship the mannequins somewhere or donate them? Dressed or naked? On and on it went. (I did learn you can donate mannequins to police departments to be used, ironically, for target practice.)

By walking them through the potential logistical nightmare and ensuing budget overruns that they were unwittingly creating, the client found their way to a different solution which involved lights and paper cut-outs still effective and much more feasible.

Sometimes people continue to hang on to a bad idea even *after* the 25-question exercise. That's when you drop what I call the "budget hammer." Save this tool for when a client wants the impossible with no regard for the insane logistics or their negative effects on the event. As people-pleasers, we and our vendors tend to turn ourselves into pretzels to make the impossible happen and then feel guilty about charging for our time. I admit we don't always pass along the full cost of these endeavors. While you may think it helps your relationship with the client it may actually be encouraging bad behavior. Charging people for tight turnarounds, overtime, and making the impossible happen serves multiple purposes:

- The cost may shock the person back to reality and eliminate the request.

- Paying for services is the way this works—we're a business, not a charity.

- If a client wants something they have to be willing to pay for it.

If a client requests additional items or work to be done within the original time-frame, but they haven't allocated additional budget, simply ask them to decide what they want to eliminate to afford the new items or which tasks they want to scrap in lieu of the new priorities. Otherwise, you're creating a monster and setting the stage for problems.

Here's my golden rule: "You must not care more about an event than the people paying for it do."

We were thrilled to land an event with a very well-known telecommunications provider. We imagined that the partnership would be long and mutually fulfilling. One usually does.

We met with the planning committee, which was comprised of people from numerous departments. The conversation somehow turned to whose turn it would be to bring hangers for their own coat closets for the event. One woman laughed and said she still had clothes on a chair in her room from when she'd had to pull all her clothes off the hangers last year. Huh?! My team and I were dumbfounded. This blue-chip company was expecting their employees to supply hangers for the event's coat room? We didn't have much time to dwell on that when the discussion turned to who would pay for the mints and hard candies that they wanted to put on the meeting room tables. Apparently, there was no money for those either. Really?!

That's an extreme, but 100% true, example. We were appalled, but this had become normal for the company's internal planners. We cared about fairness more than the stakeholders did. It was clear that this was just one of many other problems in how this organization did things. We completed the event, but it was a "one and done" experience for my team. Though it proved to be enormously educational on what *not* to do!

There are times when no matter how much logic you throw at a situation, the crazy holds on tight. That's when it's time for you to revisit your own goals and decide if you're in the right place and if what you're doing is serving *you*. If it's not, then it may be time to move along. If you stay, consider that you may have your own matching brand of crazy.

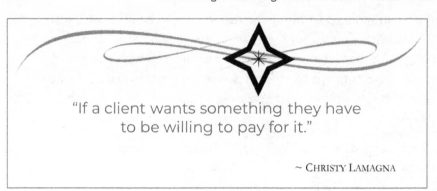

"If a client wants something they have
to be willing to pay for it."

~ Christy Lamagna

CHAPTER NINETEEN

Nurturing a Curious Mind

"Think and wonder. Wonder and think."

~DR. SEUSS

Key Terms for This Chapter:

✧ Curious Mind

✧ Curious Mind Exercise™

When the impossible looks easy, you can be sure that the plan behind it is covered with mental fingerprints. Usually, the correlation between the seeming ease of a task corresponds directly to the intensity and scope of the planning.

The cognitive ability to simultaneously think in opposing directions is a trait great leaders possess. Be it corporate tycoons, generals in the armed forces, or chess grand masters. Each thinks many steps ahead about multiple variables, attaches a probability to the various potential outcomes, dissects the situation for its components and influencers, formulates action options, and creates both forward and contingency plans with confidence. I call it, having a "**curious mind.**"

Most successful event strategists have curious minds although they may not realize it or identify that in themselves. They instinctively dissect program elements into small parts, analyze them, ask questions surrounding them, consider what could go wrong, determine how to reduce risks, figure out how to handle challenges and then put it all back together and act. They know from experience that small details, when neglected or overlooked, can become huge problems in no time.

Near the beginning of the semester in the strategic planning course that I teach, I told my students that any gathering could be considered an event and therefore, would require thinking through the details. To put their skills to a test, I asked them to plan a pizza party for the following week's class. They'd be graded on how well it unfolded. They all thought it was a guaranteed "A." After 15 minutes of class time, all 18 students agreed that they'd thought it through thoroughly and were done planning.

By the following week pizza and soda were ordered, and supplies were purchased according the plans they'd made. The person who'd picked up the six pizzas and the soda couldn't carry it all in one trip, so she delivered the first three pizzas and a couple of two-liter bottles of soda. Then she had to walk back to her car for the rest. (This campus is notorious for its scarce parking, so the trip to her car and back was a seven-minute errand.)

Once she returned and the boxes and bottles were opened, people began to serve themselves. They quickly realized they hadn't ordered enough non-meat options. This caused some grumbling and some mitigating pepperoni removal. They had plates, but they didn't have cups! And what about paper towels and spray cleaner to get the dripped pizza grease off the desks? They'd forgotten to buy those, too.

Fortunately, I had done this exercise before. Under my desk, I had a cooler with ice, cups, paper plates, paper towels, and cleaning supplies. When it came time to tally the expenses and divvy up the costs, they also realized they didn't have enough singles to make change. I'd anticipated that also and brought a stack of one-dollar bills.

A simple pizza party proved to be full of elusive details and hidden costs. The students were surprised. They realized they could have anticipated and avoided these oversights with a bit more thought (and perhaps more pizza-party experience). They understood the lesson: There is more to a flawless event than meets the eye.

Event strategists draw on their experience and context awareness to determine what logistics to manage and how to make the event seem effortless. (That's our gift!) Planning events has been compared to ducks swimming: It appears graceful and effortless...until you look below the surface.

That's why I created the "**Curious Mind Exercise**." Because planning graceful, elegant events is anything *but* effortless. These exercises help strategists refine their critical thinking skills. Doing so is the equivalent of taking out a mental insurance policy.

You also must remember that you're not planning alone. It takes teamwork. And, frankly, the smarter the people around you are, the better you can do your job.

✧ Here are examples of some of the exercises to help you pay attention to important details:

- Choose an object at random, something from your briefcase, your desk, or that's visible from your window. For two minutes, write down as many questions you can think of about that item. Now that your mind is limbered up, do the same exercise, but this time apply a strategic planner perspective.

- Consider a task you do without thinking, brush your teeth, tie your shoes, eat an ice cream cone, and write down every step necessary to accomplish the task. Test yourself by doing the task just following your list and see what you missed.

Mastering Strategy

Event strategists who aspire to become Master Strategists need to go another step beyond logistics and synthesize information at a much higher level. They have to anticipate the impact of disparate, apparently unrelated world events on their events. Here's a Curious Mind Exercise to work that mental muscle:

✧ Choose a headline from the newspaper. For instance, take these headlines:

- "Gas Prices Expected to Rise due to OPEC Supply Cut"
- "World-Series Victory Parade Scheduled for Monday"
- "Three-time Olympic Gold Medal Winner Convicted of Drug Use"

What could these headlines have to do with events? If you put your curious mind to work on this problem using an event filter, you can broaden your perspective while keeping events at the center. This way, you can start to assess the relationships and potential points of impact. For instance,

- "Gas Prices Expected to Rise due to OPEC Supply Cut"
  - Gas prices rising can negatively affect attendance at an event for an external audience that may be driving to the event.
  - Airlines impose fuel surcharges when prices either spike or remain gradually on the rise.
  - Your transportation budget may need to be adjusted to accommodate a fuel surcharge, delays, or cancellations that you didn't anticipate.
- World-Series Victory Parade Scheduled for Monday
  - The parade may cause road closures that may make it impossible for attendees to get to your event (that was scheduled long before the city's World Series victory was even anticipated).
  - Your external-facing event attendance may drop dramatically as a result of traffic or if your audience members are also baseball fans and get distracted.
  - What arrangements can you make with hotels to substitute part of your room block if necessary to accommodate victory visitors in case your attendance suffers to avoid unnecessary room charges?
- "Three-time Olympic Gold Medal Winner Convicted of Drug Use"
  - You were expecting that Olympiad to make an appearance at your fundraiser event.
  - What contracted appearances are being canceled and what kind of scramble is happening to find replacements?
  - Where is that person's image appearing for promotional purposes, what is being done to remove it from collateral,

and how much will it cost to replace it with the substitute celebrity?

You Don't Know What You Don't Know

Logistics is not just about executing a set of tasks; it's about thinking through an array of good and bad scenarios that could occur and developing multiple contingency plans to cover them. Ask questions—lots of questions—to help you figure out what, in a given circumstance, you may be missing or what could happen.

I often ask colleagues, clients, and interviewees, "What should I have asked you that I may not have?" or "What do I need to know that we haven't covered?" Keep front and center the adage "You don't know what you don't know." It helps to open your mind to the possibility that you have overlooked something critical.

When every program element ties back to the achievement of the overall event goal, any disruptions, hiccups, or flat-out epic fails are more than inconvenient, they can be costly mistakes that hit beyond the wallet. Putting an enhanced emphasis on details and trusting that no detail is too small, will work well in your favor, trust me.

"There is more to a flawless event than meets the eye."

~ Christy Lamagna

CHAPTER TWENTY

Let's Talk Logistics

"If you don't have time to do it right,
when will you have time to do it over?"

~JOHN WOODEN

Key Terms for This Chapter:

✧ Request for Collaboration® (RFC)

Managing logistics doesn't lose its importance in the world of strategic planning. Details are still what can make or break an event no matter how brilliant the strategy. Executing details meticulously is truly an art form.

Strategic planning by no means replaces or undermines the need for brilliant logistical execution. It's true that Discovery Sessions and the Discovery Process put logistics on hold until the strategic plan is firmly in place. But you need to pick them back up once the strategy is established.

When all decisions are weighed against, "will this lead us closer to our goal," your work process is streamlined, and you can optimize your budget allocations. Depending on your starting point, this may mean budget increases, reallocations, or self-directed reductions. In today's event environment, when budgets are reduced it's often an indication of a lack of support. In a strategic environment, it's a sign that dollars are being reallocated and applied to where they are most necessary. An expenditure that doesn't support the goals should be removed or reallocated. That doesn't mean eliminating décor or florals. It means choosing elements that create the right environment to support the event's goals.

Having an executive team focused on the goals, a team you can rely on and work with harmoniously, allows you to concentrate on what's important and what you do well: maximizing the attendee experience and influencing behavior.

Requests for Collaboration

In a strategic environment, requests for proposals (RFPs) become obsolete; they're yesterday's tools. If you're going to leverage the expertise of your event partners, stop sending them templates limited to dates and space needs. Instead set up a meeting for what I call a **"request for collaboration,"** or **RFC**.

RFPs are complete when a contract is agreed upon and signed, traditionally by the planner and the director of sales. An RFC, by contrast, is an ongoing series of interactions that encourage creative thinking and where multiple parties are welcome to participate.

To start a collaborative session, explain the event's goals and ask how the space can be best utilized, instead of focusing on the logistics first. When a venue understands what you want to accomplish and is willing (and able) to help you achieve success, it's a much more engaging piece of business for everyone. It's certainly more interesting for the venue than the cut-and-paste sales meetings for which they likely receive a dozen RFPs a week.

As I write this book in the summer of 2018, it's a strong seller's market—space is limited and pricey, and the venues control the terms. But the value of repeat business never wanes. If you present a venue with the opportunity to collaborate and build an experience—one that may be repeated multiple times if successful—you will get their attention. They will be more responsive when they can have a greater role in the planning process and can establish a solid foundation on which to host repeat events. Remember the reason we go through the Discovery Process; if you ask people for their ideas and opinions, not only will they share them, they become invested in the process and the outcome. This builds stronger relationships, validates their experience and opinions, and enhances what comes out of the conversations.

Site Visits: Small Investment, Huge Payoff

Once your company is operating from a strategic perspective, there will be no need to discuss whether site visits are useful. You will be able to sidestep the top three reasons most planners give for not conducting in-person site visits:

- Budget restrictions
- Time restrictions
- The misconception that technology and word of mouth will suffice

What about using technology? It's hard to find a hotel or venue that doesn't have a website full of photos, maps, a virtual tour and other details galore.

Couple this with online reviews and Google Earth, and you should be able to paint a pretty complete picture of a place without leaving your desk, right? Hold on.

I agree that these tools can certainly provide a convenient way to gather *some* information on cities, services, and venues. But believing in online tours and Yelp reviews only is taking a big risk. Trust me. *Nothing* substitutes for physically going there. Only when you experience the destination, the environment, the sights, sounds, and smells can you determine if it's the right choice for your group. You or someone from your team must get on a plane and see the place first hand.

Remember, online photos only show the place at its best; they've been enhanced using all the tricks of modern photo editing. Anything that isn't a selling point is excluded—a flood zone, a dangerous intersection, buzzing power lines, the biker bar next door. I urge you to learn from my mistake:

I joined this industry by talking my way into the job at a startup. We all wore many hats and figured stuff out on the fly. We helped each other as best we could, but mostly we were overwhelmed. I'd had limited event experience, but that already put me miles ahead of some of my colleagues.

We had staff on both coasts; the home office was in New York. For me, that meant most meetings were local. For the West Coast team, that meant very early morning phone calls and a lot more travel. The West Coast offices were a mystery to us. We decided to host a meeting in San Francisco and didn't have much time between the decision and the event date. Anxious to make a good impression, I pulled out a destination guide and found a venue with great photos. The salesperson was friendly and helpful and promised the space was perfect for our group. There was no time for a site visit, and no one insisted we do one. The rates and dates worked, so I signed the contract.

In all fairness, everything the salesperson told me about the hotel was true. The property fit our needs, had been recently refurbished and served wonderful food. What she hadn't told me (and I had failed to ask), was that there was a row of adult movie houses directly across the street. All of them did a robust, late-night business, which I only learned about the evening we arrived to set up for the event. Wow. Talk about finding out much too much, much too late. There was nothing I could do. We just tried to keep everyone focused and busy. And I learned my lesson. Since then, I always do site visits. I've even flown from New York to San Francisco and back on the same day. Brutal as that was, it is well worth it to avoid that horrible sick feeling I had when I saw those movie theaters. There have been many times that my effort to see a property with my own eyes has saved my company and my clients from what could have been a big mistake.

Setting your Sights on Site Visits

The best way to conduct a site visit is to do all you can to mirror what your attendees' experience will be as closely as possible. Arrive at the destination airport at the same time as you expect most attendees to land so you get a sense of the traffic, the airport signage, any construction or transportation issues, etc. This may inspire a change to the event start time, an alternative route, or an entirely different venue. If you expect that your attendees will check a bag, do the same. If it takes an unreasonable amount of time to get your bags (my home airport of Newark is notorious for waits of 30 minutes or more), that's good to know and share with the client and build into the arrival instructions.

Once you get to the venue, make sure you give yourself ample time to look around and gather the info you need. For any hotel you're seriously considering, stay for at least one night. Walk around the lobby, check out the bar and the restrooms. Look in the corners for dust or neglect. For a comprehensive list of things to look for while on a site, visit the Strategic Resource Library.

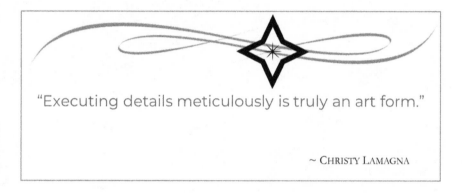

"Executing details meticulously is truly an art form."

~ CHRISTY LAMAGNA

CHAPTER TWENTY-ONE

To Be (a Good Person) or Not to Be

"Do the right thing. It will gratify some people and astonish the rest."

~MARK TWAIN

Key Terms for This Chapter:

✧ Familiarization "Fam" Trip

One of the many challenges of working in an industry that doesn't have formally established standards is the fuzziness of the line between right and wrong. It's largely left up to individuals to define based on the situation. Not all of us follow the same moral compass when locating the "true north" of integrity. Rationalizing is an easy thing to do, especially if you're in a professional environment that you feel does not appreciate your commitment and hard work. Have you ever found yourself thinking along these lines: "My boss doesn't treat me well, so I should take whatever perks I can get?" or, "If someone is offering me something nice, how can taking it be unethical?"

Most people can instinctively sense right from wrong. Though sometimes a lack of knowledge or understanding is responsible for bad choices people make—imagine you're in a foreign country and don't know the language or the customs. Those tasked with planning their organization's events as a secondary responsibility to doing their full-time job may not be exposed to industry discussions about ethics. They may believe receiving a free iPad for booking a specific hotel is a customary industry courtesy.

It is easy to imagine that a room upgrade, especially if you're on a site visit, is a harmless, well-deserved perk. But remember, you're there to mirror the experience of your clients and attendees. You arranged to stay at a property overnight to execute a proper site inspection and experience the facilities as they will; both are reasons not to take an upgrade. If you don't experience the hotel in the same way your guests will, you're wasting your site-visit time and the hotel's resources. Site visits are not vacations. The hotel will want to spoil you. This is one of those "it's the thought that counts" moments. Thank them but ask that they keep you in a standard room. Suggest instead that they send a plate of cookies or a basket of fruit, ideally with a $25 cap, as you will likely send these to your VIPs onsite.

Hoteliers are besieged with requests from planners for free rooms at properties they'll likely never book, discounts for friends and family, free spa treatments, special discounts for weddings, and more. If you're working, staying on property a day after a program finishes to decompress, or arranging to get a friends and family rate if your kids join you at the end of the event is, in my opinion, acceptable. Asking for a free room in Tahiti for your two-week vacation, just because your company books business with a hotel chain, isn't.

The lines can get a little blurry in the privacy of our own minds. When the same situation is exposed to the bright light of scrutiny, things may look very different. For instance, is it ethical to accept an invitation to be a guest on a **familiarization** or **"fam" trip** somewhere, if you have no plans to visit that location for a business event? Some justify this by thinking, how can I recommend a destination if I haven't experienced it? For me, it is justifiable if I can definitively say there is a realistic chance I will bring business to the destination or location within the next two years, AND, I tell the fam organizer that I have no current plans to bring a group to the destination or location and they welcome me anyway.

I've had numerous fam invites to visit Dubai and Australia. I politely decline the invitations with regrets. Both are places I want to see, but I have no foreseeable program requests for either area. Many people think that if they're invited, then there are no other considerations around attending. Fams are expensive for the venue and take significant time to coordinate. They cost the organizer money and occupy space that perhaps should go to someone who may be bringing business to the region or venue soon.

What about those planners who do choose to take perks because they feel underappreciated? While there is no guarantee that holding a position of respect equates to someone acting with integrity, my optimistic hope is that those inclined to take the low road will opt out of this industry. All ships rise with the tide.

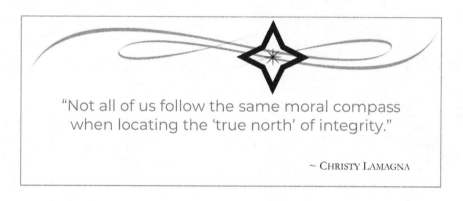

"Not all of us follow the same moral compass when locating the 'true north' of integrity."

~ Christy Lamagna

CHAPTER TWENTY-TWO

Strategy and Struggle

*"It is amazing what you can accomplish if
you do not care who gets the credit."*

~HARRY TRUMAN

Can't We All Just Get Along?

Most event professionals are take-charge, Type-A personalities. We get things done without being asked, are natural leaders and like to be right. We consider ourselves more than competent. That personality type works well until someone just like us enters the room.

One of the biggest challenges planners report in the workplace is interoffice power struggles and territorial battles. We have a lot of preconceived ideas about people's motives. If someone is overly eager to take on work and volunteer for tasks during meetings, they are often regarded with distrust. Instead of appreciating their offer to help, we become suspicious they're vying for someone's (aka our) job. During meetings, participants are hesitant to share ideas if they're concerned that someone else will steal them. When ideas are shared with "too much" enthusiasm, it is often considered grandstanding. We put ourselves and each other in no-win situations that create angst and unhappiness.

I think we sometimes forget that we have a finite amount of energy to expend each day. Supporting others generates energy. Competing with and resenting each other saps it and usually at a faster rate than simply doing our jobs.

Once you master strategic thinking it spills over into all aspects of your life. This means focusing on goals and eliminating distractions, taking emotion out of decisions, and remembering that other people's actions and behavior are not about you. But don't go too far. Don't let that backfire. Strategic thinking should also create space for new dynamics with coworkers and colleagues. It takes teamwork to achieve results.

Kathy is in the beauty parlor business. She has invited me to a few of her industry events and I'm always eager to go because everyone is so warm and genuine. Ideas and best practices flow freely, compliments fill the air, and moments of inspiration and encouragement are generously shared. It's an enormous love fest complete with shrieks of joy and "Oh my gosh, you look AMAZING!" as people rush towards each other from across the room. A stranger is simply a friend they haven't met yet. I was always greeted with enthusiasm. I overheard plenty of discussions on how one person could help, support, and encourage another or they were figuring out ways to help each other.

How refreshing! Does that sound like any meeting industry event you've been to lately? By contrast, the mood at event industry functions reflects the silo mentality. Sure, people who already know me greet me warmly. But strangers are typically ignored. You could be a competitor or someone trying to sell me something. Either way, they rarely want anything to do with someone new. Such an odd way of behaving, especially since we're in the business of bringing people together to share information and cement relationships.

In early 2000, I was the director of Corporate Events and Travel for a tech company in Silicon Valley. I managed a global team with a budget of more than $5 million a year in event spend. We did great work, were well paid and, for the most part, loved what we did. Then the dot.com bubble burst followed by the events of 9/11. The economy crashed and burned and our industry tanked. I lost my entire team to layoffs. I was crushed. Between survivor's guilt and the uncertainty of the company's future, it was a difficult time.

Prior to this, an independent planner had been calling me for months looking for work. I had had a full staff and didn't need help, but I had invited her to check back every few months. She called an hour after I'd had to let my last remaining team member go. I was a wreck. I shared with her what had just happened. Her response was a bubbly, "GREAT! We can finally work together!"

When I caught my breath, I told her how offended I was by her insensitivity. Oh, she didn't mean it that way. She apologized profusely. She even sent flowers the next day. I did hire her for a few small projects that surfaced. But I will never forget that moment nor how it made me feel.

Some say it's because we're focused on logistics rather than people or attendees rather than colleagues. Perhaps we're distracted by business operations issues and it's keeping us from being present and available. Any, or all, of that may be true, but it doesn't make for a pleasant experience nor does it move us forward as an industry. While we're working on improving how we are treated as professionals, let's focus some attention inward and be mindful of how we treat those around us. If we're all headed to the same goal, it shouldn't matter who gets the credit. I know it's idealistic and there are people in your organization who you likely simply can't stand. You're focusing on the long game; with a strategic plan in place most of the folks who are currently making your life difficult will have a choice to make; get with the program or find a new place to work. Also, worth noting; if you're one of the people who make other people's lives miserable you need to start making some changes. There's no room for ego in this process.

"Supporting others generates energy."

~ Christy Lamagna

CHAPTER TWENTY-THREE

Money, Money, Money!

"Whoever said money doesn't buy happiness doesn't know where to shop"

~BO DEREK

Key Terms for This Chapter:

- ◇ Speaker's Bureau
- ◇ City Wide
- ◇ On Consumption
- ◇ Pre-con
- ◇ SWAG

We've explored how you can get your executive team interested in adopting a strategic-meetings initiative using data. Remember the WIIFM principle? The more examples you have, the stronger your position. What you will be suggesting will seem like it will completely up-end the current system. The current system may, in fact, not be working all that well for everyone, but it still makes people nervous to confront the "way we've always done it." It's going to take data and an exertion of positive energy to break the inertia and get people moving in a new direction.

I recommend that you shine spotlights on as many opportunities to save or make money as you can. That is gold for business people. You can start by identifying innovative ways to garner free publicity and tap new markets, customers, or sponsors to bolster your argument.

Meeting Deadlines Saves Money

For some reason, executives rarely take event deadlines seriously, despite getting regular updates on critical decision dates from their event *planners*. When a *strategist* joins the stakeholder team that no longer happens and here's why. Meeting deadlines quite simply reduce unnecessary costs. By tracking savings and contrasting your current budget with those from previous years, you can identify and document beneficial spending-pattern changes that can be attributed to applying strategy to events. Demonstrating the fiscal upside of having a Master Strategist on the executive team reinforces your approach and validates your being there going forward.

Tapping Untapped Resources

Like **speaker's bureaus**, convention and visitors' bureaus (CVBs), are often an overlooked or underutilized information resource. In fact, these not-for-profit organizations *exist* to provide planners with information, access to help, and expertise at no cost. How many of us have wished for an extra set of hands but didn't have the money to pay for it? Well, CVBs are there and waiting for you to ask for their help.

Reportedly, half of CVBs are funded by hotels, restaurants, and attractions that support these organizations' activities. The other half are funded by government, often through tourism or occupancy taxes (the taxes you see on hotel bills). In either case, CVBs exist to showcase a city, help you navigate it, and provide the best experience possible for you and your attendees.

CVBs can advise on tax rebates and any incentives offered by local government to attract tourism business. These can put dollars back into your budget. Their staff can help plan your site visits and will sometimes pay for site-inspection airfare if the business you're bringing is lucrative enough. They know the hot spots as well as the off-the-beaten-path options and will even make calls. They can follow up with vendors and provide options you may not know existed. All with no hit to your budget. Using a CVB seems like a no-brainer, right? And here are ten more reasons provided by one of my favorite people, the magnificent Rick Hud, of San Francisco Travel:

✧ CVBs can:

- Assist with attaining special government permits
- Request that the city's mayor write a welcome letter to your group
- Arrange appointments to see venues and meet vendors
- Alert you to scheduled airport or roadway construction
- Source an RFP on your behalf
- Identify restaurants that are within walking distance, allow buyouts, have private rooms, and are large enough for your group
- Recommend local options for transportation, décor, staffing, DMCs, artists, entertainment or whatever else you may need
- Identify when major political or sporting events may conflict with your desired dates
- Share details about which airport is best, what airlines fly in, who flies direct, how many flights are there per day, or whether other forms of transportation are preferable
- Provide immediate details of scheduled **"city-wide"** events, sometimes scheduled years in advance

When planners hear "city-wide," they often dismiss the potential dates immediately. When a large group takes over a town, it's understood that it drives up rates and suppresses off-site venue inventory. A closer look and a curious mind will reveal there are also a few benefits to booking during city-wide (or over-the-shoulder) dates that you may not have considered:

- If your event requires a large amount of meeting space but no sleeping rooms this may be the perfect complement to city-wide events. They are typically held at convention centers but leave other area meeting spaces unoccupied.
- Your audience may be in town for the other event, which can make it more convenient for them to attend yours before or after

- Your prospects may have come to town for the other event, which gives members of your executive team the opportunity to meet with them while they're convened in a single location, saving you time and money

- If another event will be in town at the same time and their agenda is posted online, see who their speakers are. If any are compatible with your event, you may be able to negotiate a lower rate since they a will already be local.

Everything Counts

Ordering "**on consumption**" is a standard practice where you pay only for what guests consume. The items most commonly ordered on consumption are single-serve beverages, packaged protein, granola or candy bars, individual boxes of breakfast cereal, and bags of chips and nuts. I occasionally have success getting whole fruit and hard-boiled eggs added to that list and, once in awhile, tea bags, which surprisingly can save a ton of money. No matter how great you are at finding items you can serve on a consumption basis, you're potentially throwing away considerable revenue if you stop there.

It's important (and cost efficient) to check details. Traditionally, the venue's banquet team tallies what was consumed and adds the totals to the banquet checks, which the event team reviews and signs off on each day. When we see that the on-consumption counts are not round numbers, it's a good indicator they were counted, and we'd signed off on the check. However, I always have my team track the consumption numbers independently from the venue's efforts. Often we found that the counts did not match. This is typically not intentional; it is simply human error and can amount to a lot of unnecessary costs.

Here's how we strategically track our onsite consumption and better manage the client budget. While working with our client services manager (CSM) to design menus, our food and beverage (F&B) lead details what items we want on consumption. That's when we explain that our onsite F&B lead, who ideally is the same person who designed the menus, will be working with the venue's banquet team throughout the event and will be tracking on-consumption items.

Our F&B lead also attends the **pre-con** and is responsible for reviewing the food portion of the BEOs. This is our second opportunity to formally mention our policy on working with the banquet team on the on-consumption counts. We traditionally request an off-line meeting immediately following the pre-con to review the plan in detail. During that meeting, we methodically outline what we'll be doing to share our on-consumption tracking sheets. We clearly outline what we expect and how we prefer to handle deviations from the agreed-upon plan.

The F&B lead works with the venue's banquet team from the first setup of the day to the final beverage check in the staff office, often late into the night. Each time on-consumption items are put out, both parties do a count, noting how many of each item was placed. After each refresh, the count is adjusted with what was replenished and the numbers are shared between the F&B lead and the venue team. If the venue team can't do the counts because our requests are pulling them away for other tasks, then we do the calculations solely. We substantiate our numbers with pictures.

When we review the banquet checks, if there are any discrepancies between our count and the stated totals, our numbers win every time. Visit the Strategic Resource Library for a copy of our On Consumption form, which I encourage you to use. We've saved clients up to $12,000 on a single event by tracking actual consumption versus what was reported on the banquet checks. This more than pays for our headcount.

As mentioned, tea, as well as coffee, can constitute a big budget line item if you aren't careful. Not knowing how many gallons of hot water and coffee have been consumed versus what is listed on your BEOs can add up to hundreds of dollars each day. At a recent event in (expensive) San Francisco, we were charged a whopping $160 a gallon for hot water and coffee. You can avoid this sticker shock by establishing that no hot beverages be replaced without the F&B lead's sign-off; you not only avoid paying for beverages that are not consumed, you also prevent new coffee from being poured atop the old stuff (yuck!).

Free Publicity

Earning and establishing a positive reputation wherever you go is wonderful public relations. Strategically design your event to leave a positive imprint on the city you're in and simultaneously help residents and organizations. On a side note: Once you get into the habit of incorporating corporate social responsibility (CSR) into your programs, you're likely to find it the most rewarding part of your job. The options are endless and the endorphin rush from helping others is truly addictive.

One easy way to save money and make the world a better place might surprise you. Instead of renting color printers for an event or shipping them from home, just purchase them and have them delivered to your staff office at the venue. Printers are inexpensive, and most office-supply stores offer free shipping. Then, when the event is over, donate the printers to venue staffers who did an incredible job or to a local school, homeless shelter, or community organizations of your choice. Your company gets the tax write-off, avoids return shipping costs, and, let's face it, any time you ship delicate tech equipment, it's a crap shoot as to whether it will arrive in working condition anyway.

The same "give it a second life" philosophy applies to florals, extra giveaway items, and office supplies. If shipping items home costs more than they're worth, donate them. A box of paper clips may mean nothing to you, but it might be tremendously helpful to a community center or an after-school program that can't afford office supplies.

Waste Not, Want Not

The amount of food wasted at events is staggering. Even if you single-handedly try to eat all the brownies and cookies left over from the afternoon break, you likely just can't get them all down (no, I did not try this). But don't despair. You can donate food just as easily as office supplies. Venues may not readily share this information, so have with you a copy of The Bill Emerson Good Samaritan Food Donation Act of 1996. Essentially, it "exempts those who make good faith donations of food and grocery products to nonprofit organizations that feed the hungry from liability for injuries arising from the consumption of the donated food." A complete copy of the Emerson act is located in the Strategic Resource Library or online at https://www.rescuingleftovercuisine.org/donate-food. You can also work a food donation clause into your contracts so there's no debate onsite as to what happens with unused food.

Once it's agreed that leftover food can be donated, you need to secure a place to coordinate it and have it picked up. There are many non-profit groups that will manage all the details. Beyond making a phone call to arrange the pickup time and location, there's not much more you need to do. Now that you know how simple this is, there's no reason not to make this part of your standard onsite protocol.

Pro Tip:

Food that was not put out for attendees has been known to appear in the venue's employee cafeteria, so when you're told they can't make donations, push back...hard.

If your organization wants to share the news of the donation, ask the recipient for a photo with someone from your company either in front of the organization's branded food truck or posing in front of or inside the venue. It's not uncommon to ask for a mention in the charity's newsletter and to be included on its website and social media posts. Not sure who you should donate to? Your CVB contact may be able to help find suitable charities.

Once you have a giving goal in mind, brainstorming with your team is more efficient and yields more interesting ideas than you're likely to think up on your own.

With so many companies focused on corporate social responsibility these days, you shouldn't have any trouble tying that into your strategic planning. Add a team building activity into your company's giveback pledge. You can even turn your post-show cocktail hour into a team building activity. (People tend to dislike team building exercises, but most enjoy drinking.) Create a "Beverages and Backpacks" themed happy hour, for instance.

It works like this:

Allocate a portion of your **SWAG** money (gift and giveaway budget) to buy school supplies. Create a fulfillment center in your feed-and-seat space, pre-function space or wherever it would be appropriate to set up tables piled with school supplies and backpacks. Guests can station themselves in front of a pile of supplies. Each person puts a school supply into a backpack and passes it down the line until it's stuffed and ready for the boxes at the end of the tables. Everyone enjoys the camaraderie of doing something purposeful together...over drinks!

The company gets a tax write-off, garners some great press, and creates a team building exercise that isn't met with whining and pinched expressions. If you plan these opportunities with your corporate culture, attendee profiles, and company goals in mind you're on the right track.

Generating Revenue by Sourcing Wisely

Hotel commissions are trending downward, so if you're a third-party planner and they are a significant source of your revenue, you need to get creative. If you outsource your searches, you may want to consider taking them back in-house to keep those dollars. If your sourcing company is focused only on room nights and isn't considering your ballroom's load in/load out times, early dates for staff offices, breakout and pop up rooms, and other onsite space needs, you may want to reexamine your arrangements with them. Every element of the process should operate at peak efficiency, especially when making a case for an events' ability to help support sales and contribute to the bottom line.

Mo' Money

Some hotels offer a rebate to host events, in addition to offering the sourcing company a commission. If you use a third party, this allows you to continue to support your vendor partner, outsource the work, AND put money towards a master bill credit.

To track costs more effectively, create custom expense reports for each event. Lock the cells that are associated with line items the event provides—any scheduled meals, group transport, etc. Exceptions must be signed off on at a designated executive level. This curtails costs that are often overlooked but constitute a significant amount of avoidable spend.

In our 18 years of business, the Strategic Meetings & Events team has documented over $1.5 million in cost savings and cost avoidance for our clients. Numbers don't lie; positive results speak for themselves. By documenting the value of producing events strategically, you provide the WIIFM answers your executives want to see and, in the process, move into a position of authority and influence.

Love Thy Neighbor

Exploring what other events or activities are using the same venue before, during, and immediately after your event may lead to some unexpected windfalls. Ask your CSM if they will reach out to these group(s) and put you in touch to explore ways to leverage reusable equipment or materials, find procurement economies of scale, and identify other clever ways of saving money, potentially for you and the other event producers. For instance:

- If your welcome reception is the day before another event's final night activity (or vice versa), explore duplicating décor and/or florals. If the décor is rented you each save half the delivery and pickup costs. For florals, the bill is reduced by half and you can donate the flowers to a local hospital or nursing home when you're done.

- Ask the chef what is being served at the simultaneous or bracket events. Oftentimes adding your group to another group's order will allow for bulk discounts, which means you might be able to upgrade your menu from prime rib to filet mignon.

- If the event preceding yours does not have a preferred production vendor for the ballroom extravaganza and plans to use the in-house audiovisual gear, offer to hang the lighting on your trusses. They save on load out costs and you save on load in.

Don't just think outside the box. Stand *on* that box and see further and wider than you ever have before. You've got this!

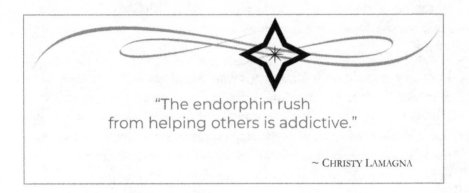

"The endorphin rush
from helping others is addictive."

~ CHRISTY LAMAGNA

CHAPTER TWENTY-FOUR

Do You Speak Speaker?

*"Tell me something new
There are stories to be told"*

~ERASURE

Speakers play a pivotal role in the strategic planning process. They deliver the content that will inspire and educate your audience, leading them toward the behavioral changes or new habits that will help reach the meeting's stated goals. With that in mind, how much time is dedicated to sharing the event goals with your speakers? Do you ever review their material in advance and, if you sense that something is amiss, offer to help? That could mean connecting them with a speech writer, a speaking coach, or a presentation deck magician. To dismiss these ideas because they would be awkward to execute is a missed opportunity.

Events for external audiences are likely to have more outside speakers, both paid and unpaid, delivering content. Internal events will probably have more internal speakers (depending on the focus and the budget). You should know how to adjust your approach to work successfully with both. Tailoring your style to prepare and support these two types of speakers is not only critical to their success, but yours as well. Ironically, it's exactly what you're expecting them to do: gear their material and delivery to the needs of the audience.

Executives may be experts in their specific departments, but that doesn't make them expert speakers. How many cringe-worthy moments have you experienced as an introverted technology or operations executive mumbled and fumbled through a presentation? Content is the fuel that will influence behavior change, but the presentation is the quality of the ride. So instead of cringing, step up and offer to help them shine, give them pointers on how to effectively drive their points home with confidence and maybe even a little panache.

I find myself needing to acknowledge, again, that while a plan may appear perfect on paper, reality can wreak havoc on perfection. We know that many executives don't create their presentations, someone else does it for them. Or if they do, then it happens just before the event. Perhaps they've even thrown together a batch of slides from other speakers and figure they'll wing it. It may be difficult to know if they'll need help.

But once strategic planning takes root, the process gets a makeover and actually becomes easier. Not everyone will comply, but for everyone who does, consider it a victory. It will become clear over time which speakers are prepared and which are skating. What will happen is that those who don't do the extra work up front will eventually realize they've slipped to the back of the pack in terms of offering perceived value to their audience. You will start to see them opting in for a rehearsal the next time around.

For 12 tips to help speakers hone their style and delivery, visit the Strategic Resource Library.

Working with Outside Speakers

If you haven't used a speaker's bureau because you think they cost too much, I'm about to make your day. Many bureaus receive commissions from the speakers, so the speaking fee remains the same for you. This is an excellent opportunity to outsource work, freeing you up to focus on your main responsibilities, and support a hospitality industry professional with no impact on your budget. It's a beautiful thing.

For a variety of articles on how to hire speakers and work with speaker's bureaus, visit the Strategic Resource Library.

Although speakers may be known for their mastery of a specific topic, encourage them to tailor their message to your audience.

To help speakers prepare for an event and its audience, I've created a checklist which can be found in the Strategic Resource Library.

"Content is the fuel that influences behavior change, but the presentation is the quality of the ride."

~ CHRISTY LAMAGNA

CHAPTER TWENTY-FIVE

Making Safety Strategic

"I've seen fire and I've seen rain"

~JAMES TAYLOR

For event strategists, an unspoken goal for every event is that no harm should come to any of its staff or attendees as a direct or indirect result of the gathering. Taking care of people onsite is our most precious responsibility. You can never think about this too much or in too much detail.

Safety 101

First, the basics. Training your team in first aid and CPR is an easy thing to put off, but it is one of the best investments of time and money you can make. The Red Cross offers training at a minimal cost, as do many local fire departments, so there are no excuses. If you've ever been in a situation where someone's life was in danger and you could do nothing to help—you should act to change that, especially as an event professional. It's a key part of the job.

I was at IMEX Frankfurt with my new acquaintance, Carl, who graciously invited me to join him for dinner. He was meeting a friend whom he dines with every year during the event, always at the same restaurant, if possible, at the same table. Carl's friend Jerry and his wife Emilia arrived, and they both greeted Carl warmly. They seemed to be close friends, as the hugs lasted longer than I would have expected for a business friendship. When they sat down, I noticed that all three had tears in their eyes. My goodness...what had happened, I wondered.

Emilia turned to me and asked if I knew how she and Jerry knew Carl and why they always had dinner at the same place every year. I admitted that I had only met Carl recently and did not. So, she explained: It was 12 years ago. She and Jerry were seated at this same table having a wonderful filet mignon dinner, when suddenly Jerry started to choke. He grabbed his throat, his face was red, and his lips started to turn blue, and Emilia began to scream. Carl, seated at a nearby table, jumped up, sprinted over to the couple, grabbed Jerry, and performed the Heimlich maneuver. Out flew the steak and Jerry was saved. They had been meeting every year since. The story gave me chills. I looked over at Carl, who smiled modestly. If he hadn't known what to do, Jerry would have died that night, and Emilia's life would have been shattered. It put into a whole new perspective on the importance of knowing what to do when someone nearby needs help.

Safety First

When you're scheduling the pre-con for your event, schedule a safety pre-con as well. Find out the hotel's standard operating procedure for sick guests, power outages, strikes, active shooters, fires, dangerous weather conditions, environmental "acts of God" and any other emergency. Understand how the staff will handle them, who will be giving directions, what the evacuation paths are, and what you should do to prevent additional injuries and save lives. You will likely find out that you should listen to instructions from trained professionals when they arrive on the scene. The instinct to take charge that serves us so well in other situations could make things worse during a genuine emergency. Above all, stay calm.

When I was teaching college, I always arrived early to set up my classroom. One evening, I was reviewing some papers when a student I didn't know walked in to my classroom. He looked out of sorts and agitated. My instinct is always to help. I invited him to have a seat, and explained my class didn't start for another 45 minutes.

Suddenly, he began to cry. He said he was missing his math test in the next room, but he couldn't go in because the other students in his class hated him. I tried to calm him down and said I would speak to his professor on his behalf.

I entered the other classroom and shared the little I knew with the professor. He said the student was emotionally disturbed and could be dangerous. He called security, but since he was mid-test with his other students, he asked me to go back and wait with the young man until security arrived. Don't ask me what I was thinking going back into my classroom. But I did it.

When I returned, my "guest" was clutching his backpack to his chest and rocking back and forth. He was muttering incoherently. I realized I was in way over my head. I continued to tell him he was safe in my room and could stay as long as he liked. Inside, I was freaking out! I checked my watch and prayed there was no gun in that backpack.

After 45 minutes, a trained counselor arrived, and I was able to scoot out as she was introducing herself. I found my class standing in the hall and escorted them into an empty classroom across the hall. My heart was still pounding as I made an excuse that our regular room had been reserved for a meeting. I learned later that state troopers had arrived and had gently but firmly escorted the student out to a waiting ambulance.

It was then I realized how unqualified I was, and had been, in handling serious emergencies. Perhaps that's true for you, too. If you're like me, you kick into gear when you encounter a lack of leadership and instinctively take charge. You're calm when a water pipe in the ballroom ceiling bursts during the welcome reception; you're calm when the Prime Minister loses his badge in the limo right before his speech; you're calm when the caterer drops the ice sculpture. But we're talking about a very different type of calm here, especially if you can manifest it when you think you might be facing death. I wasn't truly calm. Frankly, I had been reckless and stupid.

After that incident, I met with security experts, mental health workers, first responders and other professionals who respond to emergencies and gathered some best practices. Here are a few good ideas to incorporate into your safety protocol.

Know Who's Staying Where

If you contract with multiple hotels, compile a complete list of all guests with contact info and the names of the properties where they're staying (and the room numbers, if available). Book at least one team member at each host property. If there is an emergency, that person is responsible for taking action, alerting the rest of the team, and contacting other designated people to coordinate. If an evacuation is necessary, having this information gives you a jump on quickly reaching guests and making sure everyone is accounted for.

Pro Tip:

Create a simple checklist of guests that can be shared and updated by everyone in real time. Need one? Visit the Strategic Resource Library for an example.

Fire Safety

When you arrive at the venue for your site visit, make sure fire exits are clearly marked and free of obstacles. Know where the stairs are and the quickest path to safety from your group's meeting rooms as well as from your sleeping room. If you really want to hedge your bets, skip the view and stay in a room no higher than the 10th floor. Chances are that anything higher is beyond the reach of a fire ladder, which, in the U.S., typically reaches up to 105 feet.

Traveling Abroad

You can create a safety net when traveling overseas by registering for the Smart Traveler Enrollment Program (STEP) (https://step.state.gov/step/). Frequent travelers can set up an account to expedite info updates for future trips. Once registered, you will receive security updates from the nearest U.S. embassy or consulate. Even more comforting is that the embassy also knows where you are and can contact you in case of an emergency.

Have It When You Need It

Take a picture of your passport and your credit cards (front and back). If your passport is lost or stolen, having a color copy of it can be useful while you are waiting to replace the actual one. For credit cards, alert the companies that you are traveling before you leave. Make sure the photos clearly show the emergency phone numbers to call if the cards go missing. Keep electronic images on your phone (perhaps under password protection) and/or print out paper copies as backups.

Finding People on Duty During Off Hours

Murphy's Law almost guarantees that emergencies occur after business hours. Make sure your travel desk has an emergency hot line and get a designated travel manager during and after business hours. You'll also avoid waiting on hold for hours when the carriers are overloaded due to impending storms or travel disruptions. Make sure there is a plan in place to handle your group's travel should a specific person or the entire group need to change locations unexpectedly.

I located resources online to augment my company's basic safety protocols. Visit the Strategic Resource Library for a list of additional resources.

There are also a host of courses and toolkits for fire prevention, safety protocol best practices, and ways to prep for other emergencies available that are worth investigating online.

"Taking care of people onsite
is our most precious responsibility."

~ CHRISTY LAMAGNA

CHAPTER TWENTY-SIX

Onward and Upward

"To hell with circumstances. I create opportunities."

~BRUCE LEE

Key Terms for This Chapter:

✧ Intellectual Philanthropy

Well, we've come to the final chapter. I feel like I've said it all, and, at the same time, I feel like I haven't even scratched the surface.

I realize the transformation I envision requires a steep climb. As Henry Ford wisely said, "If you can only see obstacles, you have taken your eye off the goal."

Looking back over all we've discussed, I'm sure you'll agree that you have so much to gain from incorporating strategic planning into your organization and your work. Think about the many benefits that come with evolving your role from planner to strategist.

The formula for success is easy, but it will take work to effectively blend the ingredients. Remember the assessment you created about your professional life? Imagine being able to double the number of positives and significantly reduce the negatives. Armed with the principles of WIIFM to get your executives' attention, the knowledge to begin real data collection and analysis, and an extended team to support you, you are ready to start your professional transformation.

Success starts with our individual commitments, but it requires all of us to share this message. We must inspire others to follow suit and break down silos. Can we see each other as "colleagues" instead of competition? I urge you to make a promise to yourself and our industry to support, mentor, and inspire others. You will gain so much by giving, and you'll have a legion of others who want to support you. What could be better than being surrounded by people who want to help you succeed?

We must stand together when industry forces move to bully us, whether it's hotels cutting commissions or publications ignoring stories that would threaten their ad revenue stream. It means supporting the speakers you hear at conferences by finding out if they've been paid, and if not, asking the organizers why.

It means having a curious mind, not just with respect to events, but focused also on your peers, your colleagues, your industry, and the world. Imagine how much of a difference you can make to improve other people's lives and how much you will benefit if others make that same commitment to you?

Find Out More

As I shared at the beginning of this written journey: life is a series of iterations: you set goals, reach them or sometimes reset them and start anew. As I finish this book, I realize I'm doing just that. With this goal satisfied, I will now set my sights on the next three books that have been clamoring to get out of my head and onto the page.

Another goal may directly benefit you. I'm at the stage in my career when **"intellectual philanthropy"** is what motivates me, finding opportunities to share the lifetime of lessons I've learned with people at earlier stages of their lives and careers. I currently mentor six people per year to help them set and achieve goals. I plan to keep doing that. If you would like to be considered for one of those spots, please email me for more information.

Finally, I've set a goal to continue teaching and motivating others to be their best in as many ways as possible. I am also committed to filling my professional speaking calendar, publishing three more books in the next three years, producing online video courses, and leading private individual and team training. I intend to target companies that want to master the art of strategic planning. I'll also coach event professionals who want to grow into Master Strategists.

For more information on working with me or being considered for mentoring, go to: lifelivedstrategically.com or you can email me at Christy@LifeLivedStrategically(dot)com.

The Strategic Meetings & Events (SME) team continues to set and achieve its goal to design successful event experiences and environments that influence behavior and accelerate sales cycles for our clients.

To find out about hiring SME to produce your corporate events, email: WeAreListening@strategic(dot)events.

My goal to transform the industry is a big one. I am sharing it with everyone who reads my book. Whether you have a role in the hospitality or event industry, are a social planner, or know a planner who would benefit from my message, please take a moment to mention this book to them.

Let's work together to make 2028 the year that strategic planning becomes the norm. I'm focused on my objectives, but am firmly committed to seeing my strategic goal through.

I look forward to meeting you along the way and officially welcoming you to the enlightened, empowered, rewarding world of strategic events. Find me at any point in your journey. I'm happy to listen and help whenever I can.

Until the next book,

-C

"You are ready to start
your professional transformation"

~ Christy Lamagna

Glossary

Action Items: documented deliverables assigned to a specific person or department with established due dates. *Chapter 4*

Action Plan: a strategy for achieving a stated objective centered on an organization's next big moves or goals (strengthening customer focus, becoming more competitive, updating the company image, for instance). *Chapter 4*

Active Learning | The Socratic Method: participatory and interactive learning process through individual discussion and working in groups to apply what is being taught. *Chapter 8*

Audits: processes used to draw on a wide array of data collection methods including direct observation of the target audience, group and individual interviews, design excursions with key stakeholders, qualitative and quantitative analyses of survey data and more. This is the information that helps influence decisions, drives content development and achieves goals. *Chapter 6*

Banquet Event Orders (BEO): internal hotel and catering documents used to outline the menu, number of guests, special dietary instructions, meeting room set up, audio/visual requirements, and other needs associated with a catered function. *Chapter 17*

Certified Meeting Management (CMM): with a focus on strategy this three-phased executive education program includes four days of onsite education, followed by eight hours of advanced-level online coursework and a final project focused on solving a real-world, work-based problem. *Introduction*

Certified Meeting Professional (CMP): globally recognized credential. The qualifications for certification are based on professional experience, education, and a rigorous exam that focuses on four signature programs: sustainability, industry Insights, knowledge, and leadership. *Introduction*

City Wide: a convention or event so large that it will use many hotels and multiple venues. *Chapter 23*

Collecting and Connecting: a giving-based philosophy centered on finding ways to bring people together and help them achieve their goals. *Chapter 15*

Continuous Communication Cycle: ongoing, internally focused marketing program that supports learning and helps target audiences create behavior that helps an organization achieve goals and objectives. *Chapter 9*

Convention and Visitors Bureaus (CVB): a not-for-profit organization charged with representing a specific destination; most are largely funded by hotel occupancy taxes. *Chapter 17*

Corporate Social Responsibility (CSR): a business approach that contributes to sustainable development by delivering economic, social and environmental benefits for all stakeholders. *Chapter 6*

Curious Mind: term used to describe a strategist that thinks many steps ahead about multiple variables; attaches a probability to the various potential outcomes; dissects the situation for its components and influencers; formulates action options, and creates both forward and contingency plans with confidence. *Chapter 19*

Curious Mind Exercise: an exercise designed to sharpen awareness, build curiosity, and heighten one's ability to connect the dots thereby forming meaningful conclusions. *Chapter 19*

Data Discovery: a process by which critical audience information is gathered and used in the creation of content and the event design process. *Chapter 2*

Destination Management Company (DMC): a professional services company with local knowledge, expertise and resources, working in the design and implementation of events, activities, tours, transportation and program logistics. *Chapter 17*

Destination Marketing Organization (DMO): a not for profit organization charged with representing a specific destination and most are largely funded by hotel occupancy taxes. *Chapter 17*

Discovery Process: a five-step process used by event strategists to determine event objectives. Steps include: master discovery sessions, discovery sessions, data discovery, strategic content creation, and post-show metrics, audits and reviews. *Chapter 2*

Discovery Sessions: meetings held for each event among key stakeholders to establish how the event will meet its objective. *Chapter 2*

Ecosystem: a community of interacting people and their physical environment. *Chapter 6*

Engagement Questions: questions designed to create rapport and a level of comfort between participants before the data discovery process officially begins. *Chapter 7*

Environmental Design: the purposeful shaping of form and content to achieve desired results. *Chapter 10*

Event Design: creation, conceptual development, and staging of an event using event design principles and techniques to capture and engage the audience with a positive and meaningful experience. *Chapter 3*

Event Objectives Calendar: a document that identifies all meetings and events in a defined period of time as well as target audience, dates, location, objectives, and goals it is intended to support. *Chapter 2*

Event Planner: creates events and manages all logistics surrounding the event's execution within a budgetary framework. *Chapter 1*

Event Planning: application of project management to the creation, development, and completion of events. *Introduction*

Event Strategist: creates research-based immersive event experiences designed to fill their audience's needs. In doing so, they support and accelerate an organization's predetermined, measurable sales and marketing objectives. *Chapter 1*

Events Industry Council: a 33-member organization that represents over 103,500 individuals and 19,500 firms and properties involved in the meetings, conventions, and exhibitions industry. The Events Industry Council's vision is to be the global champion for event professionals and event industry excellence. *Introduction*

Exit Questions: questions designed to capture any angles missed during a discussion and to prompt any final suggestions or sentiments. *Chapter 7*

Experiential Design: the purposeful shaping of form and content to achieve desired results. *Chapter 10*

Exploration Questions: questions designed to get into the discussion and touch on the heart of the relevant topics. *Chapter 7*

External Audience: individuals or groups outside of an organization at whom its communications and promotional efforts are aimed. Example; clients, prospects, customers, etc. *Chapter 9*

Familiarization "Fam" Trip: a complimentary or low cost trip for travel agents or consultants, provided by a travel operator or airline as a means of promoting their destination and services. *Chapter 21*

First Right Refusal: a contractual right that gives its holder the option to enter a business transaction with the owner of something, according to specified terms, before the owner is entitled to enter into that transaction with a third party. Commonly used to hold hotel space before going to contract. *Chapter 3*

FOMO: acronym for "fear of missing out." Anxiety that an exciting or interesting event may currently be happening elsewhere, often aroused by posts seen on a social media website. *Chapter 2*

Forgetting Curve: the period just after learning has taken place when we start to forget what we have just learned. *Chapter 9*

Goals: the result or achievement toward which effort is directed., the overarching vision. *Chapter 2*

Impulse Answers: initial or impulsive responses given before someone has thoroughly thought through the question. *Chapter 4*

Intellectual Philanthropy: the practice of sharing events and experiences that inspired one's drive, the trials and tribulations experienced on one's rise to success, and the ways life's obstacles were overcome. This is done free of charge to help those who are advancing in their lives and careers. *Chapter 26*

Internal Audience: refers to individuals or groups within (or closely associated with) an organization. Example; employees, franchisees, etc. *Chapter 9*

Internal Marketing Program: ongoing marketing program which supports event communications to an internal audience. *Chapter 9*

Key Performance Indicators (KPIs): measure changes in critical, quantifiable variables - sales numbers, attendance numbers, reorder numbers - that demonstrate how effectively a company is achieving its key business objectives. *Chapter 4*

Key Stakeholders: individuals who are directly involved in the production of an event. Traditionally those whose budgets will help pay for the event. Example; sales executives, chief marketing officers, Master Strategists. *Chapter 3*

Learning Environment: refers to the diverse physical locations, contexts, and cultures in which attendees learn, bringing relevance and meaning not only to what content is presented but also to how and where it's presented. *Chapter 8*

M.I.C.E.: acronym for the Meetings, Incentives, Conferences and Exhibitions industry. *Chapter 6*

Master Discovery Session: an initial session in which goals and objectives are assigned to each event. *Chapter 2*

Master Show Deck: Final file of presentations placed in sequential order to be presented during a session. *Chapter 12*

Master Strategist: the highest level of event strategist attainable. Someone who has become fully proficient in the art of designing meetings and events that achieve business goals and objectives. *Introduction*

Meeting Design: the purposeful shaping of form and content to achieve desired results. *Chapter 10*

Meeting Objective: a specific and measurable targeted outcome that is tied to a particular business goal. Examples might include a 5% increase in the customer base, 10% fewer quality control cases, 25% faster product deliveries to the channel, etc. *Chapter 6*

Meeting Planning: is the coordination of all aspects of meetings and events including meeting location, transportation, and other details. *Chapter 8*

Meeting Professionals International (MPI): the largest meeting and event industry association worldwide. Founded in 1972, MPI provides innovative and relevant education, networking opportunities and business exchanges, and acts as a prominent voice for the promotion and growth of the industry. MPI has a global community of 60,000 meeting and event professionals including more than 17,000 engaged members and its Plan Your Meetings audience. It has more than 90 chapters and clubs in 19 countries. *Introduction*

Meetings Mean Business Coalition (MMBC): an industry-wide coalition to showcase the value that business meetings, trade shows, incentive travel, exhibitions, conferences and conventions bring to people, businesses, and communities. *Introduction*

Mindful Meetings: meetings that include mindfulness techniques to create audience focus, awareness and balance in the present moment. *Chapter 8*

Mindfulness: when the mind is fully attending to what's happening, to what you're doing, to the space you're moving through. Focusing exclusively on the moment you are in. *Chapter 8*

Objectives: specific, short-term actions that advance towards the goal. For our purposes, events are objectives. Objectives require answers to WHO, WHAT, WHEN, WHERE, WHY and HOW. *Chapter 2*

On Consumption: food and beverage billing option that charges on a per item consumed basis. *Chapter 23*

Open Ended Questions: questions that allow and encourage creative feedback. *Chapter 7*

Pain Points: information gathered during Data Discovery which determines the WHAT, as in what the target audience needs to hear, learn or do to improve performance. *Chapter 4*

Passive Learning: method of learning where participants receive information from a speaker and internalize it, and where the participant receives no feedback from the speaker. *Chapter 8*

Pop-up Meetings: unexpected meetings that arise with little to no warning. These meetings are not on the Event Objectives Calendar. *Chapter 2*

Post-mortem: a discussion (usually at the end of the project) to identify and analyze elements of a project that were successful or unsuccessful. It answers the question, "How'd we do?" *Chapter 2*

Post-show Metrics, Audits, and Reviews: data collected after an event that analyzes the effectiveness of the meeting's content, presenters, design and the overall experience. Used to create best practices and go forward improvement plans. *Chapter 2*

Pre-con: a meeting that is held with key event vendors and suppliers one or two days prior to the actual event where key elements of the event are reviewed in detail. *Chapter 23*

Production Strategist: the person responsible exclusively for the management of the ballroom, production team, show-flow, and the speakers once onsite. *Chapter 12*

Professional Convention Management Association (PCMA): a non-profit professional organization, with members in 35 countries, for people involved in the operation of conventions. Founded in Philadelphia, Pennsylvania, PCMA relocated from Birmingham, Alabama to its current headquarters in Chicago, Illinois, in 2000. PCMA has 17 chapters throughout the United States, Canada and Mexico. *Introduction*

Qualitative: relating to, measuring, or measured by the quality of something rather than its quantity. *Chapter 6*

Quantitative: relating to, measuring, or measured by the quantity of something rather than its quality. *Chapter 6*

Request for Collaboration (RFC): a discussion that reviews the needs of a proposed event and encourages creative thinking and collaboration to create a goal-driven event proposal. *Chapter 20*

Request for Proposal (RFP): a document that details the proposed events needs and solicits a proposal. *Chapter 17*

Return on Investment (ROI): the ratio between the net profit and cost resulting from an investment of some resources. A high ROI means the investment's gains compare favorably to its cost. *Chapter 6*

Smart Badges: a chip enabled badge that collects data on attendee behavior and preferences and allows for increased attendee engagement. *Chapter 1*

SMART Goals: goals that are specific, measurable, accountable, realistic and timely. *Chapter 4*

Spaced Repetition Method: learning that is spaced out over time and repeated to improve retention and recall. *Chapter 9*

Speaker's Bureau: groups that represent a collection of speakers and facilitate sourcing speakers for a variety of needs such as motivational talks, celebrity appearances, conference facilitators or keynote addresses. Traditionally offered at no cost to the strategist booking the talent. *Chapter 23*

Standard Operating Procedure (SOP): a set of step-by-step instructions compiled by an organization to help employees carry out complex routine operations. SOPs aim to achieve efficiency, quality output and uniformity of performance while reducing miscommunication and failure to comply with industry regulations. *Chapter 9*

Strategic Content Creation: relevant, timely content based on information gathered during the Data Discovery Process. Strategic content influences attendee behavior and helps an organization achieve its goals and objectives. *Chapter 2*

Strategic Meetings: research-based, immersive event experience designed to fulfill an audience's needs. In doing so it supports and accelerates an organization's predetermined, measurable sales and marketing objectives. *Chapter 6*

Strategic Objectives: a document that identifies an event's goals and target audience and is shared with all key event staff and vendors. *Chapter 17*

Strategic Plan: an organizational tool that helps to keep a company on track to meet growth and financial objectives. Strategic plans envision a desired future and translate the vision into broadly defined goals, objectives and tasks. *Chapter 2*

Strategic Planner: creates research based, immersive event experiences designed to fill their audience's needs. In doing so they support and accelerate an organization's predetermined, measurable sales and marketing objectives. *Chapter 7*

Strategic Planning: the process by a strategic planner used to create research based, immersive event experiences designed to fill their audience's needs. In doing so they support and accelerate an organization's predetermined, measurable sales and marketing objectives. *Chapter 2*

Strategic Planning Movement: A group created to bring awareness to the evolution of the event industry in a collaborative environment. *Chapter 13*

Strategic Vision Team: key stakeholders directly responsible for a meeting's outcome. These individuals usually attend invitation-only discovery sessions, many of whom would likely have also been in the Master Strategy Session. *Chapter 3*

SWAG: acronym for Stuff We All Get as related to free promotional items given to event attendees. *Chapter 23*

Target Audience: the intended audience for the content being delivered. *Chapter 3*

Tasks: are the steps or activities performed to complete the objectives. Tasks are the event logistics behind the meeting. *Chapter 2*

Voice of God (VOG): used by production, the VOG is the individual making announcements that are either pre-recorded or from the production booth during the course of the event. *Chapter 12*

WIIFM: acronym for What's in it for me. The key to what drives all human behavior. *Chapter 7*

Bibliography

Chapter Two

"Goals vs. Objectives – What's the Difference?" *Goals vs. Objectives – What's the Difference?*, InvestorWords.com, www.investorwords.com/article/goals-vs-objectives.html.

Chapter Six

Nawn, Founder, John. "Designing Meetings That Matter." *End-of-Course Smart Evaluation Template*, The Perfect Meeting, Inc., www.theperfectmeeting.com.

Chapter Seven

"Effective Focus Group Questions" Center for Innovation in Research and Teaching, https://cirt.gcu.edu/research/developmentresources/research_ready/focus_groups/effective_questions.

Chapter Eight

Gifford, Julia. "How the Most Productive People Schedule Their Day." *The Rule of 52 and 17: It's Random, But It Ups Your Productivity*, The Muse, 31 July 2014, www.themuse.com/advice/the-rule-of-52-and-17-its-random-but-it-ups-your-productivity.

Abrahams, Feraaz. "Understanding Generation Z Learning Styles in Order to Deliver Quality Learning Experiences." *Understanding Generation Z Learning Styles in Order to Deliver Quality Learning Experiences*, Precision Industries, 29 July 2015, www.precisionindustries.com.au/whats-hot-right-now-blog/understanding-generation-z-learning-styles-in-order-to-deliver-quality-learning-experiences.

Collins, Paul. "Meeting Room Configurations." *Meeting Room Configurations*, Jordan-Webb, 1 Aug. 2018, www.jordan-webb.net/downloads/meeting_room_configurations.pdf.

Duckworth, CAE, CMP, LSP, Holly. "Mindful Meetings." *The ABCs of Mindful Meetings*, Midwest Meetings, 23 May 2018, www.midwestmeetings.com/spring2018/the-abcs-of-mindful-meetings.

"What Is Mindfulness?" *What Is Mindfulness?*, Mindful, 18 June 2018, www.mindful.org/what-is-mindfulness/.

Chapter Nine

"Forgetting Curve." Wikipedia, Wikimedia Foundation, 30 May 2018, https://en.wikipedia.org/wiki/Forgetting_curve.

"Brief Diversions Vastly Improve Focus, Researchers Find." *Brief Diversions Vastly Improve Focus*, Researchers Find, ScienceDaily / Source: University of Illinois at Urbana-Champaign, 8 Feb. 2011, www.sciencedaily.com/releases/2011/02/110208131529.htm.

"Global Marketing Services Spending 2018 | Statistic." *Marketing Services Spending Worldwide from 2012 to 2018 (in Billion U.S. Dollars)*, Statista , 2018, www.statista.com/statistics/282197/global-marketing-spending/.

Lamagna, Christy, and Julian Lwin. "Designing Meetings That Matter." *Designing Meetings That Matter*, Corporate Event News, July 2018, www.corporateeventnews.com/index.php/design-experiences-elevate-brand-engagement.

Chapter Ten

Nawn, John. "What Is Meeting Design?" What Is Meeting Design?, The Perfect Meeting, Inc., 3 Apr. 2017, www.theperfectmeeting.com/2016/12/09/what-is-meeting-design/.

Lwin, Julian. "Design & Brand Experience." Design & Brand Experience, Lwin Designer, www.lwindesign.com/.

Chapter Twenty-Three

Ma, Runbai. "Donate Food." The Bill Emerson Good Samaritan Food Donation Act, Rescuing Leftover Cuisine, www.rescuingleftovercuisine.org/donate-food.

Chapter Twenty-Six

Dawson, Roger and Summey, Mike. "Why is intellectual philanthropy important?" Nightingale-Conant, http://www.nightingale.com/articles/intellectual-philanthropy/.

About the Author

Christy is the founder of and Master Strategist at Strategic Meetings & Events, an international, award-winning strategic planning firm. A lifelong learner, intellectual philanthropist and author, Christy taught college-level strategic planning for ten years which helped inspire her book, *The Strategic Planning Guide for Event Professionals*.

Forbes, *Fast Company* and *Entrepreneur* online are among the many publications that have interviewed Christy, who has also been featured in AMEX OPEN and The UPS Store videos.

For the last decade her focus has centered around disrupting the meetings industry. She is teaching planners to evolve into meeting strategists, who think with curious minds and learn to create meeting environments that achieve goals, shorten sales cycles and influence attendee's behavior.

As this book publishes Christy is already creating the outline for two new ones; the first geared toward entry level strategic planners and the other an examination of benefits gained by living life strategically.

Christy's passion for teaching extends beyond the written word. A member of the National Speakers Association (NSA), she is a sought after speaker, trainer, facilitator, and coach, sharing her insight with audiences in the event industry and beyond on topics ranging from entrepreneurship and strategic marketing to building powerful networks goal setting.

Christy is deeply committed to giving back and strives to contribute as much positive energy as she can to the world; whether it's serving on boards of not-for-profits or mentoring those who need a role model. Find her at: Christy@lifelivedstrategically.com. She'd love to hear your story and find a way to help you achieve your goals.

1) W-7 application
2) Passport
3) certified acceptance (not expired)
4) copy of tex tero return

copy of 2019 tax return

2019 & 2020 return with application

date of entry = space.

Mail to: irs.gov

IRS
wthin Itin operations
Po Box 302
Austin, TX 78714-9342

How long does it take?
9-11 weeks.

so, I can do my 2020 tax
But the 2020 tax return

el = A

great

great

lli

CPSIA information can be obtained
at www.ICGtesting.com
Printed in the USA
BVHW070953030220
571272BV00004B/336

9 781732 563827